Language across Difference

MW00328256

Once a predominantly African American city, South Vista opened the twenty-first century with a large Latino/a majority and a significant population of Pacific Islanders. Using an innovative blend of critical ethnography and social language methodologies, Paris offers the voices and experiences of South Vista youth as a window into how today's young people challenge and reinforce ethnic and linguistic difference in demographically changing urban schools and communities. The ways African American Language, Spanish, and Samoan are used within and across ethnicity in social and academic interactions, text messages, and youth-authored rap lyrics show urban young people enacting both new and old visions of pluralist cultural spaces. Paris illustrates how understanding youth communication, ethnicity, and identities in changing urban landscapes like South Vista offers crucial avenues for researchers and educators to push for more equitable schools and a more equitable society.

Django Paris is Assistant Professor of Language and Literacy in the College of Education at Michigan State University.

Language across Difference
Ethnicity, Communication, and Youth Identities in Changing Urban Schools

Django Paris

CAMBRIDGE
UNIVERSITY PRESS

CAMBRIDGE UNIVERSITY PRESS
Cambridge, New York, Melbourne, Madrid, Cape Town,
Singapore, São Paulo, Delhi, Mexico City

Cambridge University Press
The Edinburgh Building, Cambridge CB2 8RU, UK

Published in the United States of America by Cambridge University Press, New York

www.cambridge.org
Information on this title: www.cambridge.org/9781107613966

First published 2011
First paperback edition 2013

A catalogue record for this publication is available from the British Library

Library of Congress Cataloguing in Publication data
Paris, Django.
Language across difference : ethnicity, communication, and
youth identities in changing urban schools / Django Paris.
p. cm.
Includes bibliographical references and index.
ISBN 978-0-521-19337-5
1. Language and languages–Study and teaching. 2. Multicultural
education. 3. Sociolinguistics. I. Title.
P53.45P37 2011
306.44'609794–dc23
2011016715

ISBN 978-0-521-19337-5 Hardback
ISBN 978-1-107-61396-6 Paperback

For Mummums and Gumpy – you are with me in all I do

Contents

Figures

Tables

Acknowledgments

My deepest appreciation goes to the youth I call Ela, Miles, Carla, Julio, Rahul, Gloria, Rochelle, and Carlos. I learned more from each of these extraordinary young people than I could have ever hoped. They welcomed me into their lives and I spent one of the most intense years of my life sharing my days with them. I gained much more than knowledge from these youth. I gained hope, renewed dedication, and a group of amazing young friends. Their willingness to share so much with me made this book go.

I am also very thankful to all the teachers and administrators at South Vista High. They gave me access to their classrooms and to the school and allowed me to work with the youth with little interference. In particular, thanks to the teachers in the tenth grade biology class, ninth and eleventh grade humanities classes, and Spanish classes I spent so many hours observing.

I had many mentors at Stanford University who helped make this book possible. Arnetha Ball believed in my ideas from the first time I met her. She opened up the world of scholarship for me. I try to uphold her commitment to language, literacy, and justice in these pages. Andrea Lunsford read earlier versions of all the chapters in this book. She pushed me to think about the connections between power and writing, and to pen this book in my own voice. John Rickford welcomed me into the field of sociolinguistics and encouraged me to stay grounded in education. His guidance in developing the social language methods was simply critical. Guadalupe Valdés introduced me to the study of bilingualism and bilingual education. Her thoughtful comments on my thinking about language helped me immensely as I conducted this study. I have learned much about research and about curriculum from Denise Pope. She listened to me throughout my fieldwork and early writing and provided many helpful suggestions.

Professors John Baugh, Linda Darling-Hammond, Joy Williamson, Paulla Ebron, Patti Gumport, Elliot Eisner, Ray McDermott, and Bryan Brown also made important contributions to the thinking and research in this book through their teaching and through their comments on my work at Stanford. Many thanks as well to my Stanford writing group, Laurie Stapleton, Mike Dunson, and Heather Mailin.

I had the extraordinary privilege of being a fellow in the National Council of Teachers of English Cultivating New Voices among Scholars of Color program (CNV) as I worked on this study. The phenomenal group of senior and junior scholars taught me so much about conducting humanizing research. Juan Guerra, my CNV mentor, pushed me to think about the nexus of oral and written language and to focus fieldwork and writing toward an organizing theme.

I was very fortunate to receive the generous support of a fellowship from the Spencer Foundation. Beyond the considerable gift of time to write were the wonderful senior and junior scholars I met at the Spencer retreats. My thanks especially to my Spencer reading group and to Kris Gutiérrez and Marjorie Goodwin for helping me grapple with my shifting units of analysis.

I was also very fortunate to receive the generous support of a fellowship from the Ford Foundation. The Ford Foundation welcomed me into a community of scholars of color working across the disciplines on issues of social justice. I am so proud to be part of this community of scholar activists.

My thanks as well to my colleagues at Arizona State University – especially my ASU writing group, Rudy Guevarra, Kelly Jackson, Marivel Danielson, and Seline Szkupinski-Quiroga, and to Bruce Matsunaga for his expert assistance in formatting the photographs. David Kirkland at New York University was also extremely helpful in his critique of my thinking and writing in later versions of this book.

Major appreciation goes to my editors at Cambridge, Helen Barton for believing in this project from the first and for her thoughtful suggestions and support over the years and Sarah Green for her help in the later stages of production.

My mother, Coral, and my father, David, brought me up to care about social justice. My sisters, Iana and Rashida, and my brothers, Jamal and Marley, were raised in this same way. I hope I have represented this commitment in the pages that follow.

My thanks to my Godmother, Dianne, who taught me about ethnography long before I knew what it was. And to my stepfather, Steve, who taught me to question.

My aunt, Dorienne, was with me from Jamaica across the miles. Aunt D has shown me what it means to work for equity in an unequal world.

My dear friend JoJo White, taken from us far too early, taught me much about the relationship between urban youth culture and social justice.

My grandmother, Mummums, and my grandfather, Gumpy, were watching all along in the many years I worked on this book. They both taught me so much about achieving things in this world.

And finally, to Rae, who was there every day of these years to challenge and support my research, my thinking, and my writing. She encouraged me to write like the young poet she met all those years ago. And she helped me remain devoted to the issues of cultural equality at the heart of this book. Her fierce dedication to all of our people continues to show me the way.

PERMISSIONS

Versions or sections of the following chapters appeared previously in articles by the author and are reprinted here by permission:

Chapter 1 and Chapter 3: "A Friend Who Understand Fully": Notes on Humanizing Research in a Multiethnic Youth Community, *International Journal of Qualitative Studies in*

Education, Volume 24, Issue 4, June 2011, Copyright © Taylor & Francis Group, LLC.

Chapter 2: "The Second Language of the United States": Youth Perspectives on Spanish in a Changing Multiethnic Community, *Journal of Language, Identity & Education*, Volume 9, Issue 2, May 2010, Copyright © Taylor & Francis Group, LLC.

Chapter 4: "They're in My Culture, They Speak the Same Way": African American Language in Multiethnic High Schools, *Harvard Educational Review*, 79:4 (Winter 2009). Copyright © by the President and Fellows of Harvard College. All rights reserved. For more information, please visit www.harvardeducationalreview.org.

Chapter 5: Texting Identities: Lessons for Classrooms from Multiethnic Youth Space, *English Education*, Volume 42, Number 3, April 2010, Copyright 2010 by the National Council of Teachers of English.

1 Beginnings: shouts of affirmation from South Vista

It's our culture, we have to …
> – From an interview with Carlos

True Hamoz gurl fo lyph (True Samoan Girl For Life)
> – From a text written on Ela's backpack

Blacks, Mexicans, and Polynesians; we all gotta stay together …
> – From an interview with Miles

In an essay written near the end of his life and career, Pulitzer Prize winning playwright August Wilson (2000) described the motivation at the heart of his cycle of epic dramas which depict the Black experience in twentieth-century America. Wilson wrote that his characters are "continually negotiating for a position, the high ground of the battlefield, from where they might best shout an affirmation of the value and worth of their being in the face of a many-million-voice chorus that seeks to deafen and obliterate it" (p. 14). What Wilson sought to reveal in his work were these shouts of affirmation, shouts of identity and cultural worth in the face of the vastness of oppression. I seek similar revelations in this book. I seek to reveal how Carlos's belief that the cultural ways of his community had to be voiced, Ela's statement of her eternal Samoaness, and Miles' sentiment of shared marginalization were shouts of affirmation in the face of a dominant society that did not highly value the youth I worked with.[1] Beyond the considerable task of revealing youth strivings for voice, and self, and power, I also seek to understand how the processes of these strivings worked in a changing multiethnic youth community to challenge and reinforce lines of ethnic and linguistic difference. Further still, my goal is to show the ways this understanding can help us re-vision language and literacy learning in schools.

At heart, this book is about difference, division, and unity as it played out in a multiethnic high school of color during the 2006–07 school year and into the summer and fall of 2007. It is a book about a small group of youth in particular, their ways with language and text and their forging of ethnic and linguistic identities in the face of continued segregation and racism, in the face of poverty, in the face of a changing community, and in the midst of their high-school years. It is a meditation on how their shouts for affirmation of cultural worth were often at odds with the dominant societal and school expectations and how these cries for validation often went unheard. And, finally, it is a book about how the search for linguistic and cultural affirmation within and between ethnic groups at times maintained ethnic divisions and at other times created conditions for interethnic unity.

In order to provide an initial sense of the context where I pursued this understanding, let me briefly introduce the fieldsite. I conducted fieldwork primarily at South Vista High, as well as in the broader city of South Vista. I had worked in the South Vista community for three years prior to the study, engaging in research and teaching at South Vista High and at a local middle school. So although I officially conducted this study over one school year and into the fall of the following school year, I had been engaged in learning and teaching in the South Vista community for much longer.[2]

South Vista is a small city located in one of the major metropolitan areas of the West Coast of the United States. For over four decades this small city has been predominantly a community of color. From the 1960s into the 1990s, South Vista was mainly an African American city. In the 1980s the Latino/a population began to grow rapidly as immigrants flowed in from Mexico and Central America and a transformation began taking shape which continues to the present. A significant Pacific Islander population from Samoa, Tonga, and Fiji has also continued to flow into South Vista since the 1980s. In 1990 the US Census reported a population of 42% African American, 36% Latino/a, and 6% Pacific Islander. A decade later in

2000 the numbers had shifted dramatically to 59% Latino/a, 23% African American, and 8% Pacific Islander.[3] I could say much more about South Vista, about the grand history of Afrocentric education and politics there, about the lack of a supermarket or a traditional public high school, about the community leaders who continue to fight for respect and resources from the wealthy neighboring cities, about the many community organizations doing good work there, and about its years in the 1990s with one of the highest murder rates in the United States. Yet this is not a book about a city, though you will learn much about South Vista in the following pages.

South Vista High School, where I spent the bulk of my research hours, is a small public charter school serving students exclusively from South Vista. The school is the only public alternative to a busing program that takes South Vista youth into the public high schools of neighboring affluent communities. During the time of my fieldwork, all of the students at South Vista High were students of color and, like the broader community, the school was undergoing a dramatic demographic shift. Just two years before my study in 2005 the school served 55% Latino/as, 34% African Americans, and 11% Pacific Islanders. In 2007 the numbers were a startling 74% Latino/a, 16% African American, and 10% Pacific Islander.

I should note briefly that the demographic shift in this city and school are not an anomaly. Many urban communities throughout the United States are now home to larger numbers of Latino/as in addition to African Americans and other ethnic groups of color from South and Southeast Asia and the Pacific Islands (among other places).[4] African Americans, in fact, are experiencing an ever smaller urban presence in US cities and South Vista is certainly a case in point. Understanding the experiences of young people in such changing multiethnic communities and schools should be a top priority for all of us in the social sciences, particularly those concerned with language and education.

South Vista High boasts relatively high graduation and college acceptance rates. Many South Vista High students are the first in their families to graduate from high school. Almost all of those that attend college will be the first in their families to do so, and by most estimates many of these youth were headed toward becoming high-school dropouts or worse. The teachers at the school are caring, hard working, and well qualified. By standard measures of success, South Vista High is doing well. And I could go on in this positive vein.

It will be easy in the following pages to forget this early favorable characterization of South Vista High. Much of what I came to understand about language and text and difference at South Vista was not well attended to by the school. In fact, some of my most important findings about division and unity went unnoticed or were ignored in my observations of the official life of the school. Yet my critiques of what was not happening at South Vista High are not leveled at the school or the teachers. The school and the teachers were doing good work within policy constraints and macro systems of inequality, many of which were beyond their control. I have larger targets in mind, namely our urban public schools, how we prepare teachers for them and, more broadly, our societal conceptions of ethnic and linguistic difference. My critiques, then, should be read as criticisms of the vital opportunities schools and society continue to miss in multiethnic and multilingual contexts, rather than as criticisms of a single school or the dedicated adults who worked there. And yet this is also not a book about school success or failure, or of teachers and teaching, though the implications do land on the practical ground of pedagogy and curriculum.

It was the students I worked with over the year that allowed me to hear their shouts of affirmation, to glimpse the workings of difference in their school and city. I am after big things in this book, and to come even close to realizing my goals I relied on the big hearts and minds of eight young people who were my focus participants over the year. There was Ela, a fifteen-year-old Samoan who immigrated to South Vista from American Samoa just three years before my study. And there was Miles, a fifteen-year-old African American who had lived all his life in South Vista. I also worked with Carla, a fifteen-year-old Latina who immigrated to South Vista from Michoacán, Mexico at the age of three and remained undocumented during our work together. There was Julio, a seventeen-year-old Latino, who also remained undocumented during our work together, even though he had come to South Vista at the age of two from Sinaloa, Mexico. There was Rochelle, a fifteen-year-old African American, who had lived in South Vista all her life. Rahul, a fifteen-year-old Fijian Indian, had also lived his whole life in South Vista, though his Hindu parents were born and raised in Fiji. I also worked with Gloria, a Latina fourteen-year-old, who had lived nearly all her life in South Vista and the neighboring communities, though she had spent a couple of years in Michoacán in early childhood. And finally there was Carlos, a seventeen-year-old Latino, who came with his mother to South Vista from Michoacán in 1999 to join his father who had been living in South Vista since the late 1980s.

In the following pages you will come to know the ways these young people used and thought about oral and written language within and between ethnic groups at South Vista High and in their broader youth and family communities. And you will come to know how these facets of their social and cultural selves participated in reinforcing and challenging lines of ethnic difference in positive and difficult ways. You will hear, I hope, a chorus of shouts for cultural and linguistic affirmation within and across ethnicity. It is through this chorus that I attempted to understand difference, division, and unity at South Vista High, in the city of South Vista, and further, if readers will allow, in the multiethnic and multilingual fabric of American society.

DEVELOPING A HUMANIZING RESEARCH STANCE
The process of coming to understand the workings of ethnic difference with the youth in my study, of coming to hear their shouts of affirmation, involved developing a humanizing research stance

throughout my fieldwork. It will be helpful for me to introduce this stance as it allowed for much of my learning at South Vista. I will use an email I received from Rahul toward the end of my study as an initial description of this humanizing stance in ethnographic and social language research across difference.

It was late August 2007, and the new school year had just begun. During the summer I had been in contact with many of the case study youth from my study, but over two months had passed since the last day of school, since I had ended my year of ethnography and social language research with them at South Vista High. I had spent the school year at South Vista investigating the ways Carla, Miles, Julio, Gloria, Rochelle, Rahul, Carlos, Ela, and their many peers lived ethnic difference through their everyday language and literacy and theorizing with them about what these things meant for their educations and futures. Over the summer my occasional text messages, MySpace exchanges, telephone conversations, and visits with participant students continued to be very important to my understanding and relationships, but they were much less frequent than before. The intensity of my connections with these young people during the school year seemed some distance away as I worked through the summer months analyzing the ethnographic and social language data they had been so generous in sharing.

Yet, as was often the case that summer, these occasional interactions delivered powerful understandings that reverberated through my own emerging interpretations of the social, cultural, and linguistic worlds I was working to comprehend. I had spent several weeks letting the data settle and beginning to create ever-firmer categories of meaning and these summer interactions met my emerging sense-making head-on. All of these unsolicited summer interactions not only pushed my own understanding further, they also spoke to the strength of the bond the students and I had formed together. One interaction I had with Rahul spoke to this strength of relationship and, I think, to the validity of the sorts of truths youth shared with me over the year in formal interviews, informal conversations, and participant observations.[5] Rahul emailed me on August 27th, 2007, as I was sitting in my office coding interview transcripts. Rahul was a Fijian Indian emcee who regularly wrote and recorded rap lyrics, referred to as "flows" in Hip Hop culture. He ended his email with the following "freestyle," an unplanned flow displaying verbal (and here, written) agility and ingenuity.[6]

> YO MAN THIS A SPITTA
> RHYMING AND TWISTING IT UP FOR A HEAVY HITTA
> D JIZZLE IS THE MANE
> STANDING 6 4 YOU NEEDA UNDERSTANE
> HE'LL LAY YOU OUT WITH THEM KILLAWATT PUNCHES
> HE'LL TAKE A YOUNGESTER THAT COMES IN BUNCHES
> D JIZZLE IS THE ONE AND TRULY
> HE IS A FRIEND WHO UNDERTSTAND FULLY
> HE KNOWS WAT WE GO THROUGH
> CAUSE HE'S BEEN THROUH IT
> HE'S INSPIRED ME THE WAY AND TOLD ME TO DO IT, TO
> IT
> THIS FLOW WAS FOR U DJANGO ... LIL FREESTYLE FROM
> OFF TOP OF MY HEAD ...

There is much African American Language (AAL)[7] and Hip Hop Nation Language (HHNL)[8] to analyze in Rahul's rap, and I dedicate Chapter 5 to a thorough analysis of the textual worlds of South Vista's youth. My purpose in sharing these lyrics here, however, is to highlight the importance of relationship in ethnographic and linguistic anthropological research, and to give some evidence of the depth of my relationship with the youth whose worlds I have attempted in small ways to represent in this book. Deeply connected to this sense of relationship, I share Rahul's rap to show how he felt I had grasped the cultural meaning of the youth world.

In essence, Rahul's freestyle was a message to me about the trust I had gained and a message letting me know that I was getting it as right as an ethnographer can; that I was "a friend who understand fully," "Who knows wat we go through," who has "been through it." While I make no claim to coming close to fully understanding the complex linguistic and cultural world of South Vista's multiethnic youth community,[9] Rahul's rap told me that he felt I did. Gaining such insider trust and grasp of the cultural meanings of participants is the major purpose of ethnographic and cultural social language research.[10]

Rahul's line about my having "been through it" deserves further comment. I was honest with the youth about my own racial and ethnic identity as a Black/biracial man with a Black Jamaican immigrant father and a White American mother. I was honest with them about my own father's years without documents, about his spotty presence in some years of my childhood, and about how we have grown an ever-stronger relationship since my teenage years. And I told them about the years my single mother collected welfare to care for my sister and me. I was also honest that I did not grow up in the urban center like these youth – that I was born in San Francisco and returned there and to Oakland frequently to visit my father, but that I attended mainly rural public schools until college. I told the youth that my father had graduated college before he immigrated to California and that my mother was not the first in her family to graduate college when she returned in her mid-thirties to get her BA, then MA. I also told them about my years as a classroom English teacher in California, the Dominican Republic, and Arizona. This is all to say that I shared with youth the many ways we were similar and the many ways I was an outsider. And I shared each of these things over time and relationship because they asked me. They demanded that I claim identities and experiences in the ways I was continually asking them to in the somewhat dialogic process we call ethnography. This sharing of self in dialogic process, I believe, led youth to share their selves in more genuine and honest ways. This genuine and honest sharing led to richer and truer data than the model of the somewhat detached, neutral researcher that echoes across the decades from more positivist-influenced versions of inquiry in applied cultural anthropology.[11]

Rahul delivered one more important methodological message in his rap that summer day; he showed me that he felt humanized by the experience of being a research participant. Our year-long relationship, filled with formal interviews about language, ethnicity, schooling, music, and violence, filled with email exchanges and conversations about his raps, his classrooms, and the distance between the two, filled with my participant observations of him inside and outside the classroom – these ethnographic and linguistic anthropological events had been inspiring to Rahul. In the rap, he told me, "He's inspired me and told me to do it, to it." Although I did not *tell* Rahul to do anything during our year, the manner of our interactions, my questions, and my genuine search to understand his understanding made him feel inspired to "do it, to it," to keep striving in the face of many obstacles. This is the terrain of what I have come to see as *humanizing research*, a terrain I only began to explore in this study and a terrain occupied by a growing number of critical ethnographers and social language researchers. Humanizing research is a methodological stance which requires that our inquiries involve dialogic consciousness-raising and the building of relationships of dignity and care for both researchers and participants.[12] Although such a stance is important in all research, it is particularly important when researchers are working with communities that are oppressed and marginalized by systems of inequality based on race, ethnicity, class, gender, and other social and cultural categories. This ethical need for a humanizing stance emerges as both researchers and participants seek to push against inequities not only through the findings of research, but through the research act itself.

Building relationships of dignity and care and glimpsing insider understanding across multiple borders of difference was a major challenge of my research in South Vista. So, too, was attempting to conduct my study in ways that avoided exploitation and colonization, in ways that were humanizing to the youth that had gifted me with access to what they did and thought about. Rahul's rap is one piece of evidence of the ways I managed these complex border crossings somewhat successfully. Throughout this book, I will provide further examples of the way my research interactions with participants attempted to help the youth and myself toward a deepened sense of how oral and written language worked at South Vista. How my field methods allowed me in small ways to "understand fully" and, in even smaller ways, "to inspire" the youth in my study; to humanize through research rather than colonize by research.

THE NEED FOR INTERETHNIC LANGUAGE AND LITERACY RESEARCH IN US SCHOOLS

When I arrived at the fieldsite in the late summer of 2006, I came laden with particular categories of race, ethnicity, and language as they applied to Latino/a, African American, and Pacific Islander students. And I came to South Vista wanting to know how youth from each of these ethnic communities negotiated the cultural distance between their everyday practices and those of school. What became apparent within the first months of fieldwork was that such lines of ethnic and linguistic difference and division operated far differently, and in far more complicated ways than I had read about or researched as a scholar or understood as a teacher. Sure, I came with knowledge of multiple identities, cultural dissonance, and even cultural hybridity. My own life as a Black Jamaican/White American biracial man, fused with reviews of decades of literature had prepared me for that. But the intensity of solidarity, of exclusion, and of interethnic sharing in linguistic and textual practices was beyond my expectations.

As I spent more and more time in the sociocultural worlds of young people, my focus on the youth/school tension became less prominent and I began to fix my research gaze on the thriving multiethnic youth cultural space. It was here that language and literacy was practiced and contested between youth both inside and outside the classroom. It was here that youth strove for power and voice in ways so crucial to our notions of teaching and learning in multi-ethnic contexts. It was here that difference was enacted and challenged through moments of everyday interaction.

Contemporary approaches to the study of mind and culture begin with the understanding that our identities and social practices are situational, fragmented, and in a dialogic relationship with cultural context.[13] Such approaches note that in a multiethnic and increasingly global society, any notions of static or core selves and stable cultural rules are impossible. People of color in colonial, post-slavery, and other oppressed contexts as well as others marginalized by sex, gender, and class have been forced to approach cultural being in this way long before the postmodern era. Dubois (1903), for instance, conceptualized a painful *Veil* between the cultural worlds of African Americans and European Americans in the United States over a century ago. This Veil creates what Dubois termed a *double consciousness*, "a sense of always looking at oneself through the eyes of others" (p. 215). This double duty of self and culture becomes even more complex in social contexts where there is not simply one dominant and one marginalized culture (e.g., Black and White), but rather many differently marginalized cultures coexisting in a single dominant cultural setting – in this book a high school serving students of color from several ethnic backgrounds.

The multiple consciousnesses and multiple practices that can result from such a cultural space are beautifully theorized in Anzaldúa's (1987) conception of the cultural and linguistic *borderlands* as a "liminal state between worlds, in between realities, in between systems of knowledge, in between symbology systems" (Anzaldúa, quoted in an interview with Lunsford, 2004, p. 17). Although these borderlands are often places of conflict for students, like those in South Vista, who come from less powerful social positions, Anzaldúa's conception allows as well for the possibility of fluidity between belief systems and cultural practices in multiethnic contexts.

Pratt (1987, 1991) offers another way to view these borderland spaces. She envisions them as *contact zones* between individuals and communities with different cultural repertoires of language and understanding. For Pratt (and for me) understanding what occurs in these zones of contact in our multiethnic, multilingual, race, gender and class stratified world is major ground of needed knowledge in our shifting global and multiethnic world. With this in mind, Pratt (1987) envisioned

> a linguistics that focused on modes and zones of contact between dominant and dominated groups, between persons of different and multiple identities, speakers of different languages, that focused on how speakers constitute each other relationally and in difference, how they enact differences in language.
>
> (p. 60)

Most of the scholarly work done in the United States investigating the terrain of double consciousness, the borderlands, or contact zones in schools and communities has analyzed the ways such multiple identities and linguistic practices occur as a result of the tensions between dominant White middle-class ways and the ways of one particular marginalized or oppressed group (e.g., Mexican Americans or African Americans).[14] This research that is focused primarily on the linguistic and cultural negotiations of one ethnically marginalized group must continue as the historic and continuing experiences of each group in relation to the dominant expectations of school and society are indeed different. However, demographic shifts coupled with the continued residential segregation of poor communities of color in the United States have increased the numbers of Black and Brown students who share the same communities and classrooms.[15] It is common for schools and communities across urban America to be home to Latino/a, African American, and other immigrant communities of color like Pacific Islanders. South Vista High is a case in point.

It is also true that students of color – Latino/as and African Americans in particular – continue to be failed in large numbers by our public schools. Students from these communities of color continue to lead drop-out and incarceration rates and score most poorly on standardized national and state tests. We have long known from scholarship at the intersection of sociolinguistics and education that the linguistic and literate practices of communities of color must become resources for classroom pedagogy and curriculum.[16] This long line of work has pulled many researchers and teachers out of viewing the linguistic and cultural practices of marginalized ethnic groups as deficits to be overcome in classroom learning and toward understanding them as resources to be used in classroom learning.[17]

What has been less clear as a result of little sustained social language and educational research focused on US multiethnic communities, is what the resources are in such complex cultural and academic spaces and whether curricular conceptions of multiculturalism and language and literacy learning have accounted for changing communities and changing notions of difference as they are lived by students inside and outside schools. If we are interested not simply in pulling our young people into the dominant, normalizing stream of schooling, but also in re-visioning schools to allow and foster more pluralist *repertoires of practice*,[18] then we must also look carefully at the struggles for voice and power that exist between the margins of ethnicity and language in multiethnic contexts. This book is a window into the cultural and linguistic resources available in contemporary multiethnic urban schools and youth communities.

ON LANGUAGE SHARING, DEXTERITY,
AND PLURALITY

Although US scholarship has not often focused on these interethnic spaces in youth communities and schools, British Cultural Studies scholars have done important work pushing understandings of language and ethnic identity in the late modern urban contexts of Britain.[19] The work of Rampton (1995, 1998, and 2006) has been particularly important to my thinking. Very little research in the

United States or abroad has brought social language knowledge and methodology to the multiethnic youth spaces so common in contemporary urban schools like Rampton's classic (1995) ethnographic and sociolinguistic study of language use in a multiethnic youth community in Britain. His research provides a rare investigation into how language and ethnicity function among adolescents in such multiethnic space. Rampton's (2006) later work gracefully uses interactional sociolinguistic and ethnographic approaches to further understand the terrain of ethnicity, class, and language in an urban British high school.

Rampton's work moves beyond the study of bilingual ethnic in-groups and toward an understanding of what he has termed *plural ethnicities* (1998).

Working from Hall's (1988) conception of *new ethnicities*, Rampton posits that individuals can adopt plural ethnicities that challenge singular ethnicities in contexts where ethnic groups blur lines of linguistic and cultural ownership. In his analysis Rampton looked to understand the social rules of *language crossing*, moments when youth would cross into the languages of their peers during interactions.[20]

Although Rampton referred to all instances of youth employing their out-group peers' languages as "crossing," my own analysis has pointed to some moments when language was crossed into and other times when it was *shared*. While language crossing may or may not be ratified by traditional in-group speakers, I refer to *language sharing* as those momentary and sustained uses of the language that *are* ratified – when use of the language traditionally "belonging" to another group is ratified as appropriate by its traditional speakers. Such sharing occurred at South Vista when African American youth ratified the African American Language use of their Pacific Islander and Latino/a peers or when Latino/a youth ratified the Spanish use of their Pacific Islander and African American peers. This ratification was expressed by in-group speakers continuing an interaction in the heritage language with their out-group peers and, by continuing an interaction, implicitly inviting their out-group peers to continue the language sharing. Another way language crossing was ratified as language sharing was more simply when in-group youth did not protest, mock, or otherwise comment on the language sharing of their out-group peers, thereby implicitly deeming it authentic. The ways young people thought about and navigated such cultural and linguistic sharing is a major focus of this book.

While language crossing and sharing hold major implications for how we think about language, ethnicity, and schooling in multiethnic and multilingual contexts, it is important to avoid overstating what such practices can achieve in an unequal society. Although language is one primary marker of ethnicity and identity, other major markers of race, like skin color, play heavily into systems of discrimination, racism, and privilege. For this reason, I back away from thinking about "plural ethnicities" and favor more specific terms of practice, such as *linguistic dexterity* – the ability to use a range of language practices in a multiethnic and multilingual society – and terms of mind, such as *linguistic plurality*, consciousness about why and how to use such dexterity in social interactions. Such terms recognize the importance of interethnic practices without implying that they surmount systemic barriers.[21]

THE PARADOX OF PLURALISM IN
UNEQUAL SOCIETIES

My analysis, then, begins by looking at the relationship between the many marginalized linguistic and cultural practices at play among the youth I worked with at South Vista High and in the broader city of South Vista. I look to see how such practices were considered locally prestigious or not.[22] I work from an understanding of the tight relationship between language, ethnicity, and identity, a relationship that guides language choices and language attitudes, particularly in multilingual and multiethnic settings.[23] Language is seen here as an *act of identity*[24] that foregrounds particular identifications with and against others. I interrogate youth interactions for examples of local agency; small identity acts of marginalized language, literacy, and activity that resist the social order of schooling, even as they ultimately fail to eclipse its power.[25] I explore the borderlands that existed among Latino/as, African Americans, and Pacific Islanders at South Vista; the sorts of linguistic dexterities and pluralities they enacted and understood. My analysis seeks to glimpse the ways that certain types of crossings and sharings push our understandings of ethnic and linguistic division and unity and the sorts of classrooms that could use such understandings for educational improvement.

I have come to conceptualize this terrain as *multiethnic youth space,* a social and cultural space centered on youth communication within and across ethnicities – a space of contact where youth challenge and reinforce notions of difference and division through language choices and attitudes. Positioned in this research space, I analyze the forces and practices at play that reinforce ethnic divisions and those that seem to cut across those divisions toward spaces of interethnic unity.[26]

My analysis in the following chapters reveals a continuum of multiethnic youth space that explores the tensions between ethnic and linguistic solidarity and exclusion on the one end and ethnic and linguistic crossing and sharing on the other. The fundamental tension of a pluralist society lives along this continuum. The within-ethnic group practices of solidarity create safe spaces for those like you and, importantly, Other those unlike you. Such practices often perpetuate and reinforce traditional lines of difference and division even as they necessarily provide needed sustenance for particular marginalized and oppressed groups. A major necessity of a pluralist society is to bridge such lines of division so that groups can cooperate in society, while at the same time maintaining spaces for particular groups to thrive.

For oppressed and marginalized people this continues to be the major tension; a way to achieve both maintenance and access in linguistic and cultural practices. Such is the *paradox of pluralism.* It at once demands both a repertoire of difference and one of similarity.[27] Although such demands are required of all people, the more marginalized the positions that one occupies, the more difficult this is to realize. This tension between maintenance of marginalized linguistic and other cultural practices and access to dominant ones is at the heart of a century of scholarship on the struggle for marginalized people between the plural and particular, the locally prestigious and the dominant.[28]

In the United States and other nations living out the legacies of colonialism and slavery, the ground of this paradox of pluralism has generally operated between White middle-class ways as the shared and common and the ways of marginalized groups as the different and particular, though it certainly does not have to continue to be that way. At its center, this paradox is one all multiethnic societies must deal with, including the multiethnic youth communities of our high schools. How can we successfully honor both the need for difference and division and the need to unify across borders to share and understand? How can we learn to hear and heed the shouts of affirmation rising up in our schools and youth communities?

INTRODUCING THE MULTIETHNIC YOUTH SPACE OF SOUTH VISTA

JULIO: Every once in a while you do see a separation between Hispanics and Blacks, but I think it's because it comes from your family. You're used to being around just people who speak your own language or have your own style. They are like you and sometimes for some people it becomes sort of difficult to be around others. I mean, especially if they're not like you. The better someone's like you, the easier, I think, it becomes for you.

(Interview, October 23, 2006)

MILES: We're all cool. I think it's like in my [middle] school, where it was White people, and Black, Mexican and Polynesians; we all gotta stay together. I think it's like here. We all gotta stay together. We're the minorities.

(Interview, January 19, 2007)

In many ways these separate quotes from Julio, a Latino born in Mexico and raised in South Vista from age three, and Miles, an African American born and raised in South Vista, mapped out the continuum of multiethnic youth space. Julio spoke of an occasional "separation," Miles of a sense of cross-ethnic unity among youth of color. For marginalized youth living within the paradox of pluralism, both solidarity with those "who speak your own language" and crossing into spaces of common ground where "We're all the minorities" necessarily coexist. Yet, for youth in communities like South Vista, such a coexistence of in-group solidarity and cross-group commonality is highly contested and in constant tension with the linguistic and cultural demands of schooling and the broader dominant society.

Chapter 2 is about the role of Spanish language in the separations Julio spoke of between ethnic groups at South Vista. In particular, it is about the processes interlinking language, ethnicity, and identity in these separations and about how youth across ethnic groups understood and participated in these divisions in the context of a new Spanish-speaking majority. As Julio saw it, this ethnic division by language and style was a "once in a while" affair. Although I will show that such boundaries were certainly more common than occasional, Julio was aware that lines of separation were not constant or simply drawn by ethnicity and first language(s). In Chapter 2, I also explore the ways Spanish language worked to challenge and blur traditional ethnic and linguistic divisions at South Vista, creating spaces where Latino/a, African American, and Pacific Islander youth wanted to, and often did, "stay together" through Spanish.

In Chapter 3, I describe the way the Pacific Islander languages of Samoan, Tongan, Fijian, and Hindi[29] participated in the separations and togetherness of multiethnic youth space at South Vista. Although these languages were far less prominent than Spanish as tools of exclusion and solidarity in school, the chapter explores where and how these languages survived in the face of small numbers of speakers. As well, I seek to show in Chapter 3 how young people held on to fierce senses of

Samoaness and Fijianess even as they shared in linguistic and cultural practices not traditionally part of their ethnic communities.

In Chapter 4, I take up the powerful role of AAL as a cultural and linguistic unifier in the multiethnic youth space of South Vista; the myriad ways that sharing in AAL was the ultimate linguistic embodiment of Miles' statement of staying together. I show how Latino/a and Pacific Islander youth joined their Black peers in grammar, lexicon, and rhetorical traditions. I also look to complicate easy celebrations of cultural hybridity and plurality, considering the deeply marginalized position of African American youth in contemporary urban school contexts and at the positive and problematic dimensions of sharing in AAL.

In Chapter 5, I introduce the category of *identity texts*. In three interrelated sections I analyze photographs of texts worn on youth objects, texts delivered through electronic media, and rap lyrics written by youth at South Vista. I set these analyses alongside youth sense-making about the role of these texts in communicating ethnic, linguistic, and geographic identities. I end each of the chapters in the book imagining what it would mean for classrooms to engage in what I call a *pedagogy of pluralism*, using the linguistic dexterity and plurality of youth as resources for language and literacy learning within and across difference.

Chapter 6 is a meditation on the meaning of my work with the youth of South Vista for classroom learning, teacher preparation, and broader conceptions of pluralism in US society. In that chapter I seek to illustrate the ways this book offers insight into the question: how do we live and learn together in difference?

Some examples are in order to introduce the sorts of ethnic and linguistic separations and togetherness Julio, Miles, and their peers experienced daily at South Vista. Consider the following fieldnote I recorded on April 12th, 2007. Miles, Ela, Rahul, and Rochelle and many other students I knew well took Mrs. Gonzales' tenth grade biology class. The class was one of the more ethnically balanced in the school, with several African American students and Pacific Islander students joining a slight Latino/a majority. As was my custom, I sat at the back table, jotting down notes as students wrote down theirs. On this day, the class was in the middle of a long unit on DNA.

> Mrs. Gonzales is giving complicated directions to a game they will play where partners will translate duplicate strands of DNA using colored and lettered paper cards.
>
> Miles, who is shaking his head in confusion, says to nobody in particular, *"No comprende."* {He/She doesn't understand}
>
> The game begins and Miles and Derek translate the duplicate DNA code first.
>
> Miles looks up at the other groups, *"Y'all ø slow!"*[30]
>
> The groups switch roles in the game and one student, Geraldo, is confused about which role he has. Derek offers some help.
>
> Derek, "What *was* you before? You ø supposed to be over there."
>
> Miles chimes in, "You're MRNA now, *blood.*"
>
> The competition to finish heats up and Sharon yells at her Latino partner, *"¡Ándale!"* {Hurry up!}
>
> Meanwhile, in the midst of the game, Rudolfo is talking to his table mates about his flag football team. He tells them, "Sometimes people *be hittin* even though it's supposed to be flag."[31]

Such complex language exchanges were typical inside and outside of classrooms in South Vista. In just a few moments of biology class, Miles and Sharon, both African American students born and raised in South Vista, chose to cross into Spanish for a simple declarative statement (Miles, "No comprende," for the correct verb conjugation "No comprendo") to a general audience and an interjectory command (Sharon, "¡Ándale!") to a bilingual Latino peer. Both students could have said these things in some variety of English and they would have been readily understood by all in the classroom.

Within the same exchanges, Miles and African American student Derek also indexed their participation in AAL. By saying "Y'all" for "you all,"[32] using *zero copula* in "ø slow" for the Dominant American English (DAE)[33] "*are* slow," and employing the long-standing lexical item "blood" (here, for "friend"), Miles was locating himself with his youth speech community. Interestingly, Miles used "blood" to address Latino student Geraldo, even though the term has generally been used throughout its decades-old history between African Americans as a generic term for a Black person (Smitherman, 2006). Derek also used two features of AAL grammar in assisting Geraldo. First, he used the past form "was" for "were," a characteristic feature of AAL and other non-dominant Englishes using a single verb form for both plural and singular subjects in any tense.[34] Like Miles, Derek also employed a standard feature of AAL grammar by omitting the copula in "you ø supposed" (for the DAE "you *are* supposed"). Yet Miles and Derek were not alone in using AAL features during this exchange. Latino student Rudolfo used both the hallmark AAL grammatical feature the *habitual be* and the phonological feature "ing" to "in", in his statement "people *be hittin*" (for a rough DAE translation, "people are usually or always hitting").[35] Rudolfo, then, was also forging his place within the youth speech community through his use of AAL.

So hold up ... Two African American students chose Spanish for simple statements they could have made in English. Two African American students used features characteristic of AAL grammar and lexicon to address a Mexican American student. One Mexican American student, speaking to a mixed ethnicity audience, used a deep grammatical feature of AAL. And, whether the teacher heard the exchanges or not, all of this talk was done more or less within the official course of the classroom activity. Such exchanges were frequent and common across various academic and social contexts in South Vista. They seemed to push against the dominant, compartmentalized understandings of language and ethnicity which schools and curriculum, the broader society and, often, researchers perpetuate. One major goal of my work at South Vista was to begin to understand the moments when such seemingly fluid linguistic sharing happened. So I focused my collection and analysis on how youth participated in and made sense of the linguistic dexterity and linguistic plurality they embodied.

On different days in different social interactions language seemed far less shared. Where the above exchange in many ways echoed Miles' sentiment of all marginalized youth staying together, other episodes provided evidence of the separations in social language use Julio described. Take this brief interaction I recorded in my fieldnotes on September 6th, 2006, in the same biology class. On this day, the class was engaged in group work about the ecology of their community.

> Ricky is in a group with Raul, Felicia, Celia, and Paola. The three Latinas are speaking Spanish and looking at the family photos of babies and children that adorn their binders while also attending some to their school work. Ricky loud talks a couple of times that the girls are talking about babies, as if they should be focusing on something else. Then he says loudly to nobody in particular, "I can't understand what they are saying!" He looks around for some recognition, then puts his hands up high and shrugs his shoulders. The three Latinas take little notice and continue talking with each other in Spanish.

Such in-group solidarity and out-group exclusion through language use, particularly through the use of Spanish, was as common as interactions of language crossing and sharing at South Vista. Ricky attempted to "loud talk," a common speech event in African American discourse.[36] Loud talking is used to let others outside the immediate audience hear and possibly assist in influencing an interaction. Ricky was hoping for someone (a teacher, a peer, me?) to hear his talk and intercede. When this didn't work, he explicitly expressed his frustration loud enough for his group mates and others to hear. When this also failed, Ricky resorted to the gestural, throwing his hands up in exaggerated surrender. For their part, Celia, Felicia, and Paola continued their interchange of personal photos rather uninterrupted. In this brief moment, Ricky was not at all their intended audience. Solidarity and community with each other was the primary goal.

What to make of Ricky's moment of frustration? I witnessed many occasions when language kept some out and others in throughout the multiethnic youth space of South Vista. These moments were sometimes difficult to watch and I will provide some more difficult than Ricky's. As a researcher and analyst, pushing past the pain of these exclusions was often difficult. Yet, on the other side of this difficulty, I began to understand the purpose of such solidarity and exclusion as necessary for youth to maintain cherished selves in the face of dominant school demands *and* in the face of the linguistic and cultural demands of participation in multiethnic youth space. In order to stay "Black" or "Mexican" or "Poly" (the youth term for Polynesian), one had to carve out spaces and places to use the languages of those identities. In order to maintain membership in the broader multiethnic youth community, other places and spaces needed to be carved out for crossing into and sharing language and culture across difference.

All of these identities were negotiated, of course, with the dominant demands and language ideologies of school. And yet even this explanation is far from adequate. I struggled to find adequate explanations for how the extraordinary dance of language and identity was performed in the multiethnic youth space of South Vista. The remaining chapters of this book are about this dance, and about how language and literacy education can learn to join in.

2 "Spanish is becoming famous": youth perspectives on Spanish in a changing youth community

Along with the extraordinary demographic shift away from an African American majority and toward a Latino/a majority in the city and schools of South Vista came the omnipresence of the Spanish language. Spanish, spoken in various mainly Mexican varieties and in code-switching blends with varieties of English, was everywhere in youth space. By the 2006–07 school year, Spanish was at least one of the first languages of nearly 70 percent of the students of South Vista. This does not mean, of course, that it was the primary language used by all of the Latino/a youth at the school, though it was the primary home language for the vast majority of these students. In fact, as I will show in Chapter 4, many Latino/a youth participated heavily in AAL and struggled to maintain facility in the primary language of their parents and grandparents. We know little about how Latino/a, African American, and other youth in shifting communities and schools like South Vista think about and use Spanish across ethnic difference. It is to exploring this youth understanding that I dedicate this chapter.

The field of bilingualism and bilingual education is vast and it is beyond the scope of this study and my own Spanish proficiency[1] to do justice to an analysis of the proficiency levels of Spanish among South Vista youth.[2] To be sure, proficiency levels in English and Spanish varied widely, as I will show in some data examples.

Yet each of the Latino/a youth I came to know well at South Vista were all proficient enough in Spanish to converse, if they chose to, in the Spanish language with their peers, their parents, and other family members. And they were also proficient enough in Englishes to converse, if they chose to, in some variety of English with their peers in multiethnic youth space. These youth were *circumstantial bilinguals*[3] who gained facility in more than one language through the social and cultural demands of living in their South Vista community.

My goal here is to explore the ways these Spanish/English bilinguals used Spanish to exclude and include in the youth space of South Vista. In particular, I hope to shed light on the ways they made sense of such practices in relation to their ethnic, national, and local identities as "Mexicans," "Hispanics," "Latino/as," "Michoacánas," or the other various identity categories that youth claimed through participation in speaking Spanish. I also hope to shed some light on the ways non-Spanish-speaking youth at South Vista made sense of Spanish as a tool of solidarity and exclusion in their school and community. Even further, I seek to explore the ways exclusion through Spanish fostered the desire for and practices of language crossing and sharing in Spanish among African American and Pacific Islander youth.

"IT'S OUR CULTURE, WE HAVE TO": SPANISH AS A TOOL OF SOLIDARITY AND EXCLUSION

Let me return for a moment to the example of Ricky and his statement, "I can't understand what they are saying." I heard such statements often from African American and Pacific Islander youth. But were bilingual Latino/a students consciously excluding others through their use of Spanish, or were they doing so in the service of solidarity and maintenance with little attention to who was left out? It turns out both were true, that sometimes such exclusions were very conscious and other times they were not. Comments from an interview I had with Mexican American youth Carlos on March 12th, 2007, begin to explain the process. As we sat out on the bench between the athletic field and the school, Carlos explained his view about Spanish language use in his eleventh grade English class, a class serving three Black students and some twenty bilingual Latino/a students.

CARLOS: I don't think if other students in the class are speaking Spanish people should say, "Oh, don't speak Spanish, because I can't understand," because it's not our fault that you don't speak Spanish. It's just we're used to it, it's our culture, we have to. But if I was Black I would probably do the same thing. Some in the world don't speak Spanish. I understand at the same time that they wouldn't know what's happening. That's why when I'm around Black people I try to speak English as much as possible. And I'm so used to it that I switch to Spanish sometimes, but then I'll just repeat what I said in English.

Carlos's comment spoke directly to Ricky's interaction with his Latina group mates, and I did not have to prompt Carlos to come up with his imagined dialogue, "Don't speak Spanish, because I can't understand." Such statements of frustration by non-Spanish speakers were extremely common inside and outside classrooms at South Vista. The frustration of African American and Pacific Islander students at linguistic exclusion through Spanish, in fact, was a consistent factor in drawing lines of ethnic division at South Vista.

Yet frustration was only one of the factors at play in Carlos's explanation. In his scheme, using Spanish was also a tool of in-group solidarity, a vital part of his everyday repertoire, a part of "our culture" that he had no choice but to express with his Latino/a peers. This sense of Spanish as simply everyday, as an unconscious and natural practice of relationship and communication, was also a major way Latino/a youth made sense of Spanish use in multiethnic settings, regardless of consequences of out-group frustration. As Carlos mentioned, it wasn't his fault other students didn't speak Spanish; he had to.

Carlos didn't stop his explanation with the frustration of exclusion and Spanish as an everyday repertoire. He also spoke of the accommodation that many Latino/a students made on a moment-to-moment basis depending on interlocutor and social purpose. Carlos understood that some of his peers did not speak Spanish, so often switched into English completely or translated intermittently for those peers.[4] The tensions between the solidarity of "our culture," the in-group tendency toward the shared language, and the understanding that some were excluded was at the heart of the Spanish/English nexus for bilingual Latino/a students in the multiethnic youth space of South Vista.[5]

Understandings of solidarity and exclusion through Spanish use were remarkably consistent across gender among the bilingual Latino/as I interviewed. In a mid-winter interview, I asked Mexican American student Gloria about her views on Ronnie, an African American student who had transferred into her ninth grade English class in the middle of the year. For the entire second semester, Ronnie was the only non-Latino/a, and non-Spanish-speaking student in the class.

> DJANGO: And then a new student came in, Ronnie. What do you think it is like for him in that class? Because he's the only one that's not Mexican.
>
> GLORIA: Well, every time we talk Spanish he's like, "English please, I don't speak Spanish."
>
> D: What do you think about when he says that? You're just like, whatever, or do you like—
>
> G: I'm like, "Oh, shut up, you'll learn some," you know, it's like not our fault he doesn't know his Spanish. I don't talk to him in Spanish, so he shouldn't be trippin'.
>
> (Interview, February 12, 2007)

Even though Carlos and Gloria had completely different peer groups, their understandings were strikingly similar. Like Carlos, Gloria gave an example of the non-Spanish speaker frustration she heard often. She also echoed Carlos in the sentiment that exclusion was not their fault as Spanish was an everyday part of their linguistic repertoire. A final similarity was in Gloria's insistence that she didn't use Spanish with Ronnie. Even if Ronnie was present during Spanish conversations, she used English when she addressed him directly.

One additional factor in the processes of solidarity and exclusion Gloria revealed here was her belief that Ronnie would eventually learn Spanish from being in a majority Spanish-speaking youth space. This is a point I will take up later in exploring the small ways Spanish was crossed into and, at times, shared by all ethnic groups at South Vista. An example from Gloria and Ronnie's ninth grade English class helps further illustrate the complexities of solidarity, exclusion, and in-group ethnic identity through Spanish. In early February the class was working on personal turning point essays. We were in the library and the computer lab this day, as students were to type up drafts of their essays during the hour left in class. I sat jotting notes at a small table a few feet from the computer bank where the action was taking place.

Carla, Mari, Alberto, and Ronnie are sitting at the computer bank typing. The three Latino/a students are speaking Spanish, talking about how Alberto got his foot caught in the door during the last class.

RONNIE: "Y'all speak Spanish and I don't know what you're talking about."
MARI: "It's our language, we talk it."
ALBERTO: "Why don't you speak Africanese?
MARI: "And besides, you're not supposed to be understanding!"

Ronnie grins, shaking his head, and turns away to resume his typing. Alberto is still joking about his foot being caught in the door. He suddenly stumbles on a simple Spanish noun.

ALBERTO: "*Mis ... Mis ...*" (My ... My ...) He looks down at his foot, searching for the word then says, "*Mis patas.*" (My paws.)
MARI: "*Pies* (feet), you're not an animal! Just talk to me in English!" Mari shakes her head, frustrated at his Spanish.
ALBERTO: "But I like to speak my language." Reluctantly, he switches to English for the rest of the conversation.

(February 9, 2007)

This brief interaction at the computer bank provided me with a window into the major processes at play in Spanish solidarity and exclusion. Mari's response to Ronnie's frustration was that Spanish was "our language," an everyday tool of solidarity and group identity that marked who was in and who was not. Yet Mari went further here by explicitly stating that she was consciously using it to exclude Ronnie. Although English accommodation for non-speakers was common, so, too, was conscious exclusion through Spanish use. As Carlos admitted to me one day, he accommodated for non-speakers, "Unless we have something to say about them, like to each other, like between us, then that's when we say Spanish" (January 22, 2007). I came to see such moments of conscious exclusion as covert topics in Spanish.

Beyond the exclusion of Ronnie through Spanish was Alberto's comment that Ronnie should speak "Africanese." By (jokingly) using a potentially offensive name for AAL, Alberto's statement reflected two common understandings across groups. The first was that African American students did have a particular way of using language. The second and less clear here, was that Black youth should or could have a linguistic connection to Africa.[6] This tension between Latino/a students who had a mutually unintelligible language choice and African American students who did not in the same way was an obvious, but central factor in exclusion.

If the interaction had ended with Ronnie's exclusion, it would seem to fit rather tidily with the easy categories of in-group and out-group, Spanish and English, Latino/a and African American, Mexican and Black. But Alberto, who was born and raised in South Vista, was more comfortable producing English, even if his comprehension of Spanish was good. Mari and Carla, on the other hand, were both born in Mexico and had spent significant time there throughout their lives. In addition, both young women had exclusively Spanish-speaking homes. The result in this interaction was that Alberto, who was part of the Latino/a Spanish-speaking in-group that excluded Ronnie, was then himself excluded from what he called "my language." Alberto's protest showed his own struggle to connect his ethnic identity to the language he knew was an essential part of Latinoness at South Vista. In effect, his lack of Spanish proficiency cost him a moment of solidarity with his peers. There were certainly layers of struggle in such interactions. The local politics of language were often difficult for me to observe and as I write I continue to feel for Ricky, for Ronnie, and for Alberto. And I realize I run the risk in this analysis of siding with Ronnie or Alberto as the victims of exclusion and frustration. Such struggle, however, had a very positive flip side. For one, it encouraged those youth like Alberto to strive to maintain some facility in Spanish. More broadly, I came to understand that the very identity act of using Spanish as "our language," of seeing it as a necessary part of "our culture" (regardless of exclusion) was a vital maintenance mechanism for the South Vista Latino/a community as a whole. This mechanism reached beyond youth space and into the older generations. At base, it came down to a fear of losing Spanish and, with it, the ability to communicate between youth peers, between generations, and between countries.

"I DON'T UNDERSTAND YOU": YOUTH STRIVING TO MAINTAIN SPANISH

In an interview we had just before winter break, Carla described her fear of Spanish language loss. Carla was born in Michoacán, Mexico, came to the South Vista as a toddler, and returned to live in Michoacán for third and fourth grades after the deportation of her father. In her current life, her mother and grandparents spoke with her exclusively in Spanish. Carla, then, had past and present social networks that demanded Spanish language skills. And yet she was continually worried about the decay of her first language. I provide a lengthy excerpt from our interview to get at the connection between fear of loss and the frustration of her older family members.

CARLA: Sometimes I'm speaking in Spanish for my grandma, and then I end talking in English. She's like, "What? I don't understand you." And it's confusing, I don't know, it's just that I'm used to it, because here that's all I speak is English.

DJANGO: Right, at school?

C: Yeah, in school, and then with my brothers, they speak to me in English, and my boyfriend speaks to me in English sometimes, and sometimes in Spanish. But I told him to talk to me mostly in Spanish, because I'm kind of like forgetting how to speak well in Spanish so I don't know – my mom kind of gets mad, because there's some words that I know what they are, but I don't know how to say. And I'm forgetting how to say – like the other day I was gonna say the "loom" – I mean "moon" and I said, "moona." You know it's "*luna*" and "moon" in English. I said "moona," or "loom" – yeah, that's what I said, "moona." I was like, "Wait, is that right, 'moona'?"

D: And what did your mom say?

C: My mom was like, "'Moona'? It's '*luna*'!" I was like, "Oh yeah, '*luna*'."

D: And does your mom ever speak to you in English, or no?

C: No, she doesn't know how to speak any English.

(December 2, 2007)

Carla's admission that she was forgetting "how to speak well in Spanish" was echoed by many Latino/a youth at South Vista who had lived in the community for several years. So, too, were her accounts of grandparents and parents being frustrated by the English speaking of their children.[7] I was reminded again and again during the year of the pain of the Mexicana mother in Cisneros's (1989) classic novel, *The House on Mango Street*, when she hears her baby begin to pick up English: "No speak English, she says to the child who is singing in the language that sounds like tin. No speak English, no speak English, and bubbles into tears" (p. 78).

The words Carla attributed to her grandmother are full of the same frustration and pain as those of Cisneros's character. And they were amazingly similar to those of Ricky and Ronnie, though Carla is describing an exclusion of adults through English use instead of other youth through Spanish use. It is important that Carla felt the need to take explicit action to maintain her native language. Asking her boyfriend to speak with her in Spanish was a small act of linguistic agency within the centralizing forces of DAE and other Englishes demanded in her peer groups and in classrooms.[8] This agency, I believe, was connected to a pride in the Spanish language reflected in the practices and understandings of all the Latino/a youth I worked with. Simply put, the language was the primary marker of ethnic identity. To lose it would be to lose touch with a cherished self.[9]

Although the example Carla gave is a simple one ("moona" for "luna"), like Alberto, she was tripped up on a basic noun and it stood out to her and to her Spanish-speaking audience. Her example spoke to the larger issue for many Latino/a bilingual youth at South Vista: forging identities as both members of their ethnic community and as members of the broader youth community required prowess in multiple ways with language. It required at one moment the ability to draw lines of ethnic difference through language and at other times the ability to cut across them.

I should note that Spanish was in no danger of being lost to the community as a whole. The constant flow of immigrants to South Vista High and into the city assured Spanish a prominent role for the foreseeable future.[10] In addition, Latino/a youth and Spanish-speaking community networks outside school were dense and often removed from English monolinguals. I observed this first hand when Carlos invited my wife, Rae, and me to his house for a dance party he was throwing. Of the some forty youth at the party, all except one African American girl were Latino/a and bilingual.

Yet, for Carla and for Alberto, the need to maintain and use Spanish in multiethnic youth space and in communication with adults in the community as an ethnic identity act was real and pressing. In an interview with Julio, whose parents also spoke very little English, he explained the connection between pride for language and culture, the advantages of bilingualism, the need to know Spanish to communicate with elders, and the role of those elders in language maintenance.

> JULIO: I feel you can't lose your culture. It's sad because a lot of parents think it's okay not to teach their kids their natural language and, I mean, I feel language has so much history around it for kids not to learn it. Because there are people willing to pay just to learn it, and you're willing to just leave it and let it go? Not cool.
>
> DJANGO: And so if you had kids in the future, you'd want them to know Spanish?
>
> JULIO: Yeah, I wouldn't really speak to them in English because it's kinda showing disrespect, I feel. I mean, how am I gonna feel like my mom comes in and she's talking to them in Spanish and they just look at her like, "What's she saying?" I'm gonna be kinda frustrated. I can't have my parents come because my kids won't understand them, or I can't have our parents have a conversation with their grandkids?
>
> (January 26, 2007)

Spanish for Julio and his Latino/a peers was about cultural identity; a connection to history, to community, to family, and to self. Julio used his own parents' Spanish dominance to forecast his language choices with his imagined children. He did not want to lose his culture or show disrespect.

"THEY TALKING ABOUT US": MISTRUST AND SCHOOL FRIENDSHIPS

Many African American and Pacific Islander students, like Ricky and Ronnie, did not see or understand the many reasons Spanish was used as a tool of solidarity at South Vista. They did not always think about the others in the community, namely Spanish-dominant Latino/a elders, who experienced frustration and exclusion through English use that was similar to their own through Spanish use. For them, it often boiled down to their own frustrations at being excluded from exchanges of oral communication. In fact, in addition to feeling excluded, many students had developed mistrust that Latino/a youth were talking poorly about them whenever they spoke Spanish. This mistrust sometimes spilled over into verbal confrontations. Rochelle, an African American young woman, spoke of this mistrust between African Americans and Latino/as in one of our early interviews.

> ROCHELLE: Black and Mexicans, it's easy for them to get into an argument. They think that we don't know what they're saying but we do. Because Spanish is just like English, but it's backwards. And then I know Spanish because my cousin taught me Spanish. It's hecka easy to learn and they be like, "*Ooh, carrai, da, da, da*" [approximates Spanish phonology with nonsense words]. And I'm like "What did you say?" And they like "oh, nothing" … But when they're talking in Spanish they shouldn't look straight at us because that gives us a reason to know that they talking about us.
>
> (October 30, 2006)

Rochelle's comment was multilayered. At one level she claimed to know Spanish, a claim that was not true. Several times over the year she mentioned this ability and each time I tried out her claim by asking her to produce or translate simple sentences in Spanish. She could not, nor did she ever use Spanish in my observations. Rochelle's insight into Spanish syntax, "Spanish is just like English, only backwards," did show her effort at understanding, though. Although on the surface it may seem that Rochelle's false claims, her use of approximated Spanish phonology, and her characterization of Spanish as "backwards" could be simply enacting dominant language ideologies about the superiority of English, for African American and Pacific Islander students at South Vista such statements belied their own experiences of communicative inadequacy.[11] In fact, underlying this claim of knowing Spanish and other similar statements from non-Spanish-speaking youth at South Vista was an intense desire to know Spanish in this majority Latino/a school and community which I take up later in this chapter.

At another level, Rochelle's understanding of Spanish as a tool of exclusion was about mistrust. Rochelle and other youth talked often of reading Latino/a youths' eyes and body language to see if they were being talked about and disrespected. And to be sure, Rochelle's mistrust was sometimes warranted.

Using gender as an analytic lens in addition to language and ethnicity is helpful here to draw a further distinction in perceptions of linguistic exclusion by non-Spanish speakers. Male African American and Pacific Islander youth in my work usually assumed that Latino/as were not talking about them while female youth, like Rochelle, often assumed they were. Contrast these two comments from separate interviews with Miles and Fijian Indian student, Rahul, with those of Rochelle. In both interviews I was asking about each young man's experiences in Latino/a majority classrooms.

> DJANGO: Do they speak a lot of Spanish in that class or not?
> MILES: Yeah, they do. I can understand what they're saying.
> They don't talk about me in Spanish because they know better.
> (January 19, 2007)

> DJANGO: Just like whenever you're in a group and the students are speaking Spanish.
> RAHUL: See, I don't really mind. I don't really bother, you know.
> I don't really feel like they're talking about me.
> (October 27, 2006)

In neither interview did I ask if Miles or Rahul thought Latino/as were talking about them in Spanish. Yet both mentioned it to me. Miles, like Rochelle, claimed facility in Spanish comprehension. Although Miles did have some very basic conversational skills in Spanish, he did not understand the bulk of conversations in Spanish. His claim was akin to Rochelle's; it was a coping mechanism to stave off frustration. Miles also added an inferred physical threat, a typical masculine move at South Vista.

The point remains that these male youth did not assume they were being talked about. That is, there was a gender difference in assumptions here that spoke to a broader pattern of interethnic relationship, or *ethnic geography*, at South Vista. Miles and Rahul, like the majority of African American and Pacific Islander young men at South Vista, had some significant school friendships with Latinos. Rochelle and Ela, like the majority of African American and Pacific Islander young women at South Vista, had significant school friendships within those two ethnic groups, but very few with Latinas.[12] This difference in school relationships not only showed up here as heightened mistrust and tension about Spanish use, but also in the ways the bilingual Latinos at South Vista participated in AAL more than their Latina peers.

This social reality of African American and Pacific Islander young women's inter-group friendships at school and the lack of such bonds with their Latina peers at school were somewhat troubling to me. Language, mainly the Spanish language, was one factor, but it did not seem to divide young men in these groups as persistently at school. Although I will puzzle through this dilemma more in this and following chapters, we certainly need research specifically focused on the relationships, linguistic and otherwise, between Latina and African American young women as they commonly share the same schools and neighborhoods.

To be clear, this does not mean all non-Spanish speakers, regardless of gender, did not experience mistrust and talk about wanting to know what was being said, but that the assumptions for females and males in my work were often different. I should also mention that the practice of female youth at South Vista talking about other female youth and assuming others were talking about them transcended ethnicity and language. My interview data with Carla, Rochelle, and Gloria in particular is laden with such talk, as are my fieldnotes.[13] Yet language and ethnic difference heightened such concerns among young women, drawing stark lines of division, and mistrust was added to the more common response of linguistic frustration. As Rochelle said, "Blacks and Mexicans, it's easy for them to get into an argument." And, again, it was not as if Rochelle's mistrust had no basis; covert topics were certainly a part of the Spanish solidarity and exclusion matrix.

I began this chapter on perspectives of Spanish in a Latino/a majority youth community by analyzing quotes from Carlos and Gloria. One of the primary explanations for using Spanish around Pacific Islander and African American youth in these quotes was that it was simply an everyday repertoire. Recall Carlos, "We have to." Although frustration and mistrust at being excluded was real, many non-Spanish-speaking young people also understood this everyday repertoire; that such solidarity and exclusion was something that ethnic groups did if they could. Black students, of course, were the only population at South Vista that did not have the option of using a completely unintelligible language with their in-group.[14] Miles explained this understanding as we sat alone in the gym one day waiting out a mid-winter rain storm.

> MILES: For me, personally, I really don't care that they talk Spanish. If I talked in a different language, like a totally different language that they could not understand, I would talk to them, to my people, too. I wouldn't just talk English so they wouldn't know what I'm saying. Because if I talk Ebonics and they didn't understand anything I was saying, you know, then it'd be a different story. People, Black people wouldn't mind but we really speak English, we don't speak African anymore. So we can't really communicate in our own way. I guess they're mad about that. I'm not trippin over it.
>
> (January 19, 2007)

Miles saw that Latino/a youth at South Vista had the advantage of an everyday language that was unintelligible to him and his Black and Pacific Islander peers. Sure, Miles often wished he knew what was being said in Spanish, but he also knew the importance of talking to your own ethnic in-group in a way distinct from others. In his estimation, if African Americans had their own completely mutually unintelligible language, they would have practiced the same sorts of solidarity and exclusion as his Latino/a peers. It is striking that Miles, like Alberto's "Africanese" crack, linked the distinct language he did speak to Africa. He called this language "Ebonics," but realized it was not "African anymore." In fact, he realized it was not even his "own way" anymore. Such theorizing about Black language and the linguistic practices that accompanied it was a major focus of my work at South Vista. I will return in depth to processes of AAL crossing and sharing in Chapter 4.

It was impossible to miss the treasured and contested nature of Spanish in the multiethnic youth space of South Vista. I spent many hours watching the way Spanish was used to include and exclude among the young people I spent the year with. And I spent many more hours talking with youth about how they understood these things. My analysis, evidenced through the words and deeds of South Vista youth, showed the forces of family, history, and ethnic identity pulling Latino/a youth toward Spanish use and the forces of multiethnic peer groups pushing them, at times, to accommodate to Englishes. From the perspective of non-speakers, Spanish was primarily a tool of exclusion, whether purposeful or not. They sometimes viewed this exclusion as malicious, and other times as a natural fact of a multilingual community. Table 1 details the major processes in my analysis of Spanish solidarity, exclusion, and maintenance between youth at South Vista.

"I'M TRYING TO LEARN": SHARING IN SPANISH AT SOUTH VISTA

I had seen Spanish use and learning by African American and Pacific Islander students at other times during the year. And the young people in my work had told me about these practices in their ever complex explanations. And yet, as is often the case in ethnography,

Table 1. *Spanish solidarity, exclusion, and maintenance*

Processes	Examples
Everyday repertoire	It's just we're used to it, it's our culture, we have to – Carlos
Fear of loss	I'm kind of forgetting how to speak well in Spanish – Carla
Accommodation	I don't talk to him in Spanish – Gloria
Frustration	I don't understand anything they're saying – Ronnie
Mistrust	They shouldn't look straight at us because that gives us a reason to know that they talking about us – Rochelle
Covert topics	Unless we have something to say about them, then that's when we say Spanish – Carlos

a key to the cultural web of a place is revealed more deeply through a single interaction. So it was as I sat observing African American student Jamal and Latina student Veronica in eleventh grade English class. The teacher, herself a bilingual Latina, was presenting an essay format using an overhead projector.

> TEACHER: "We are following a certain style that we think will help prepare you for college."
> (Veronica, a Latina student sitting next to Jamal, sneezes loudly)
> TEACHER: "¡*Salud!*"
> JAMAL TURNS TO VERONICA: "She say, 'Salute'?"
> VERONICA: "*Salud.*"
> Jamal whispers, "What's that mean?"
> "Bless you," Veronica whispers back.
> Jamal nods his head and says quietly, "'*Salud*,' 'bless you,' ok."
> (Thirty minutes of teacher lecture and student note taking later, Veronica sneezes again)

TEACHER: "*¡Salud, mija!*" {Bless you, my daughter/dear!}
    Jamal says loudly, "*¡Salud!*" and nods his head looking at
    Veronica with a smile.

(January 16, 2007)

Jamal was one of two African American students in this class. The rest of the students as well as the teacher were bilingual Latino/as. This classroom, then, was a prime environment for frustration and mistrust. On this occasion, in this moment, however, Jamal rejected the frustration of not understanding and chose to ask, to learn, and to use.

What were the factors involved in Jamal's choice? Why did he use the word "Salud" thirty minutes after learning it? What was the social purpose of his learning and use? What did Veronica and her Latino/a peers think of such small acts of crossing or sharing in Spanish? As I tracked these questions, I came to understand something about African American and Pacific Islander desire to learn Spanish, the conditions when these small Spanish crossings and sharings occurred, and how youth viewed such Spanish use. It turned out to be significant, for instance, that Jamal made this linguistic effort with Veronica. Flirting between African American young men and Latina youth was one primary area of Spanish sharing generally ratified by the Latina in-group speakers. Latinas ratified such use as sharing by continuing the interactions and not protesting the Spanish use of their African American male peers. Jamal saw Veronica's second sneeze as a chance to show he was listening and learning, to show he was willing to make an effort to understand and speak a language he knew was important to Veronica and her community.

Many times over the year African American and Pacific Islander students told me of their desire to speak Spanish. I asked Carlos about his perspective on this African American and Pacific Islander desire.

CARLOS: It's like when we come to the United States and we
    don't speak English, we want to learn English. That's the same

thing with them. And they don't even have the government to [make them learn]. There's a lot of Latinos here, so they need to.

(March 12, 2007)

Carlos equated the importance of knowing Spanish for Pacific Islander and African American youth with the need to know English for immigrants coming to the United States. Although this is an overstatement in terms of the relative power of English over the opportunities of new immigrants, Carlos's larger point was that without Spanish, youth missed out on much of South Vista's social world.

No student exhibited this desire more clearly than Rochelle, whose claim that she could understand and speak Spanish was one way of softening the disappointment and frustration at being left out of a major artery of communication. Miles, Samoan student Ela, and Rahul also exhibited this desire as the flip side of frustration and exclusion. In fact, all the non-Spanish-speaking youth I talked to informally and formally spoke of wanting to know Spanish. Beyond this general desire, gender again seemed a particularly important factor in the way desire translated into practice in youth space. In my January interview with Ela, she spoke of her difficulty with Spanish despite a desire to learn.

> ELA: I'm not like racist, but I can't hang around with them, the way they speak.
> DJANGO: Do you like the way they speak?
> E: Yeah.
> D: What do you mean?
> E: You know the words, "*Da, la, la,*" [Approximates Spanish phonology with nonsense words] it's almost funny the way they speak like that.
> D: Right, right. But you say you'd like to learn how to speak Spanish.
> E: But I can't learn.
> D: You've tried?
> E: I've tried, but I keep forgetting how to speak.

(January 16, 2007)

Ela spoke here of the way the Spanish language was a major factor in keeping her from socializing with her Latino/a peers. This was a common refrain in understandings of solidarity and exclusion. At the same time, Ela also wanted to learn Spanish and, like Rochelle, made a weak attempt at approximating Spanish phonology. Like Rochelle's comments I discussed earlier, it is important not to see these statements as solely mirroring the dominant language ideologies other researchers have attributed to some White middle-class speakers of English.[15] In the context of South Vista, the Spanish language was needed for full access in the community and Ela, Rochelle, and their peers knew this. Yet Ela stated here and in our later interviews that she could not learn Spanish despite her efforts. Spanish, of course, was offered as a class at the school. Ela, who was enrolled in Spanish class all year, did not feel she was learning the Spanish language that surrounded her in youth space and in her community. In fact, I only witnessed one moment of Ela learning and using Spanish in youth space. During this interaction in her biology class, Ela was looking for an insult to hurl at Latino student Rudolfo who had been bothering her. She turned to her Latino/a table mates Juan and Patricia for help.

> "How do you say 'muscle' in Spanish?"
> Patricia and Juan in unison say, "*Músculo.*"
> Ela laughs and turns to Rudolfo, "You don't got no *músculo!*"
> They all chuckle.
> (January 24, 2007)

This was a rare example of Spanish learning and sharing for Ela and for African American and Pacific Islander young women in general in my observations. This lack of use fell in line with a broader gendered pattern of interethnic relationships I discussed earlier in this chapter. To be clear, this did not mean that these young women did not want to know and use Spanish, but that in my observations they had less peer interaction where such learning and use might occur.

Deeper understandings of why the young women in these two groups did not often forge strong friendships is certainly an important area of research and the current research literature on language, ethnicity, and exclusion among girls does not yet provide adequate explanations.[16] One possible explanation is that these young women were simply passive and did not assert themselves into forging relationships across language and ethnicity in the same ways young men did. I believe such an interpretation would be rather male and dominant, though.[17] I did not know any of the young women in my work as passive in their uses of language or in their social relationships. I find a more compelling interpretation of the lack of relationships and the lack of Spanish crossing as attempts by these young women to enact in-group solidarity through their choice of friends (and boyfriends). While this in-group solidarity reinforced ethnic division, it can also be seen as a mechanism of cultural maintenance. Somewhat ironically, while staying divided from their Latina peers may have been a move for in-group sustenance, it also cost Pacific Islander and African American girls the social contacts to use and learn Spanish in the small ways the young men in their ethnic groups did.

Many African American and Pacific Islander young men, on the other hand, had at least some Latinos in their school social networks. Both Rahul and Miles, for instance, talked with me about their opportunities to learn Spanish from Latino friends. Rahul spoke about this attempt to learn from his friends during our October interview.

RAHUL: Actually, sometimes, when they talk Spanish, I try to learn what they're saying, you know. So that's what I learn from them. And they kind of giggle or laugh, it must obviously be something funny. So that's how I learn, too.

DJANGO: So sometimes when they're talking Spanish you kind of are trying to listen?

R: Yeah. I'm not trying to be nosey. But I can just kind of get a little hint of what they're trying to say. Because some words in English kind of sound like some words in Spanish.

(October 27, 2006)

In our conversations Rahul often spoke of the Spanish use of his peers as an opportunity to learn a language he wanted badly to know. Although he reported being excluded from conversations even among his peers, he chose to attempt to read the social situation and garner linguistic clues rather than to turn away. Yet even for Rahul, who counted several Latinos as close friends and could be seen hanging out with them often between classes, truly learning Spanish remained elusive, an unfulfilled desire. He related this to me in our later January interview.

> RAHUL: I think it's really good, learning another language, because it's hard but it's worth it, because Spanish is like the second language of the United States. You gotta learn Spanish in everything. I used to speak Spanish too, a lot. This'll be like my third language, tell you the truth. But I didn't have Spanish between fourth to eighth grade, because they cut it off. So I just lost all my Spanish language talent. And it's hard to learn Spanish right now for me. Even though I grew up in a Hispanic community, it's very hard. It's hard to be learning it, but it's important, you know? I'm learning it little by little.
>
> (January 10, 2007)

Unlike Ela, who did not hold out a lot of hope of learning Spanish, Rahul remained hopeful that he would. I believe Rahul's hope stemmed in large part from the fact that he interacted with Latinos daily who he knew well and cared for, who were his friends. To never understand the heritage language of his friends and to be forever locked out of certain interactions was not a possibility Rahul wanted to consider. He also saw that Spanish was a necessary language in the United States and in his predominantly Latino/a community. Even with these factors buoying his aspirations to learn, Rahul felt it was hard for him. He told me of the Spanish classes in his South Vista elementary school from Kindergarten to fourth grade. He claimed that living in a "Hispanic community" coupled with these early classes had given him a sense of having some Spanish proficiency at a young age. Sadly, these classes had been cut during his middle school years. Only now in high school had he begun taking Spanish again, and so had begun the difficult process of "learning it little by little." Rahul would sometimes try his fledgling Spanish out with his peers in the guise of joking. I asked him if he used his learning with his friends later in the same interview.

> DJANGO: I know you have some Mexican friends that you hang out with – do you ever try out your Spanish with them?
> RAHUL: Yeah, always. Always trying to say something funny, you know? "Hey, *¿Por qué, amigo?*{why, friend}" you know, all that stuff? Try to say funny stuff, get them cracking up.
> D: Does it work?
> R: Yeah, it does. Always. Like, "Aw, look at this Fijian trying to speak Spanish." But they know I'm just playing around and stuff.
>
> (January 10, 2007)

Rahul reported here that his attempts to use Spanish with male peers were often in the context of joking. He was not secure enough to throw many phrases or words out as serious communication, so he tried them within the frame of humor. Although I did observe Rahul use simple words like "gracias" {thank you} as genuine communicative bridges, most of his use was indeed around joking and expletives. His jokes were a sort of *mock Spanish*[18] use common in the crossing of African American and Pacific Islander young men. Yet mock uses like Rahul's were often ratified and enjoyed as genuine humor by Latino/a peers. By ratified I mean that the Latino Spanish-speaking in-group accepted these mock uses as part of everyday peer interaction and did not seek to regulate or dissuade such uses (even though they had the power to do so). Although I will show other mock Spanish uses that were not ratified, this humorous mock use extends previous discussions on the topic that argue all mock Spanish uses are negative. That is, within the contexts of South Vista, Spanish was not simply being made fun of from a dominant to marginalized perspective. Rahul, for example, was often one of the only non-Spanish speakers in his peer group and his uses of Spanish were meant to bond him with his peers rather than set him apart. In this sense, Rahul's joking in Spanish was not simply language crossing, but ratified language sharing.

Miles also had several fairly close Latino friends at school. I asked him about his use of Spanish words, a use I had observed several times over my months in youth space. In his answer Miles explained that learning key words from his Latino peers would allow him to know if they were talking about him and stave off the mistrust of Spanish exclusion.

> DJANGO: When do you use [Spanish words], with who, like why?
> MILES: Like the Mexicans. I learn Spanish sometimes, like if
> I'm with them. You know, they teach me words, the cool ones
> teach me words, at least. Like Juan, you know, Junior. Those
> kind of people. My homeboys. They teach me Spanish, so just
> in case somebody gonna talk about me, then I'll understand
> the word. I know what they're saying.
>
> (March 26, 2007)

And indeed Miles had learned many words and phrases from his Latino peers that he used in exchanges at South Vista. In fact, Miles showed the full range of *speech acts*[19] in Spanish language crossing and sharing I observed mainly among African American and Pacific Islander young men. Like all speech acts, these acts of crossing and sharing were made with particular speaker intentions within particular norms of communication. In the following paragraphs I will use Miles' words and deeds to further explore these processes at South Vista.

Miles, like Jamal and many other African American young men in my observations, shared in Spanish to flirt with Latina youth. The following example of this use occurred as we were getting ready for basketball practice one day. Miles was dribbling a ball on the sideline next to Latina player Sonia.

Sonia is looking at Miles and smiling as he dribbles the ball.
Miles looks directly at Sonia, smiles, and says rather softly,
"*¿Qué quieres?*" {What do you want?} Sonia seems a little
thrown by his Spanish use and says, "What?" Miles repeats
himself, still smiling, "*¿Qué quieres?*" Sonia smiles more
broadly and looks him up and down. Miles chuckles, "*Oh, I
know what you want.*"

(November 27, 2006)

Miles asked his question in Spanish for effect and, after a moment of
surprise, seemed to get the desired result: more attention from Sonia.
Miles talked about this inter-language flirting in one of our interviews. I asked him about a conversation I had witnessed between
him and Julio the week before where Julio was teaching Miles some
phrases to use to impress Latinas.

DJANGO: Have you ever actually said anything to a girl in
Spanish?

MILES: Yeah, yeah, not like to meet a girl, but Mexican girls that
I already know, flirt with them, and then I say stuff in Spanish
and that helps. When you're Black and you say it in Spanish,
that helps a lot, which you know. But I've never picked up a
girl, like, saying stuff in Spanish, because I might just make
myself look like a fool, not knowing what I'm saying. So I just
say it to people I know that if I mess up, they [know] I ain't
messing up to be mean or something.

(January 19, 2007)

Miles commented that the social purpose of this type of sharing
in Spanish was to "flirt with them." As a speech act, then, the primary goal was to foster romantic allure. Miles saw that as a young
African American man, using Spanish helped his efforts. But Miles
and his peers did not haphazardly throw around such flirtatious uses
of Spanish. You had to know the young women in case your Spanish
was incorrect or unintelligible. That way you could avoid disrespect

as she would know you were trying to impress her through sharing in her language rather than trying to mock her language in a negative way.

Miles and his peers also sometimes used Spanish as a simple cultural bridge with their Latino peers. That is, they sometimes used Spanish to show across group solidarity within their friend networks beyond simply joking. One example of this occurred as I drove Miles, Ela, and Terrence home from basketball practice.

> We are driving along the border creek between South Vista and North Vista heading toward Central Avenue. We pass two Latino youth walking home from the school. Miles puts his head out of the passenger side window and yells, "¿Cómo estás?"{How are you?} The guys look at him and give an affirmative nod as we speed by.
>
> Ela is sitting in the back seat with Miles. She laughs and says, "Man, you're a nigga. They be like, 'What's that nigga saying?'"
>
> Miles laughs in agreement, "Yeah, they be like, '¿Qué?'" {What?}

(March 21, 2007)

Miles greeted at least one of the Latino students walking on the street. This use was rather genuine and ratified as a common greeting. Interestingly, Ela regulated his Spanish sharing and reinforced the traditional ethnic and linguistic boundaries, even using an N-word to do so. As I describe in depth in Chapter 4, the N-words were used commonly in complex, resistant, and sometimes troubling ways across ethnic groups at South Vista with a full range of meanings from neutral, to positive, to derogatory (Smitherman, 2006 has listed at least eight meanings for the N-words). This particular instantiation of the N-word by Ela was not generally understood by Miles and other African American, Pacific Islander, or Latino/a youth in my study as derogatory. Miles, of course, understood and lived within the ethnic and linguistic divisions Ela attempted to redraw, though he was pushing against such traditional lines here. Nonetheless,

Miles could see the possibility of Ela's point and played along, using a Spanish word to characterize the possible reaction of his Latino peers (misusing "¿Qué?" for the more probable "¿Cómo?").

Reactions like the one Ela imagined here to African American and Pacific Islander crossing into Spanish did occur when Latino/as felt their language was being negatively mocked or misused. Although this was not the case in Miles' shouted greeting to his Latino peers, it was the case at other times in youth space. This brings me to a final type of Spanish use I observed at South Vista: unratified mock Spanish. Although Spanish as flirting, genuine bridges, and even certain mock Spanish joking was ratified as shared use, some mocking was not. As an example, I provide a rather complicated interaction between Miles and Rudolfo in biology class.

> The teacher looks over at Miles' worksheet. "Are you done?" she asks him.
>
> Miles responds, "¡Sí, es correcto mucho!"{Yes, it's a lot correct!}
>
> Rudolfo isn't having it. "Stop talking like that, you embarrass yourself." He smirks and shakes his head.
>
> Miles now really goes for mock use, "I do it-o good-o." He looks at Rudy who is still shaking his head.
>
> (January 31, 2007)

Miles did not start this exchange off with a purposeful mock use. His response to his bilingual Latina teacher, in fact, was a good effort at using Spanish, though using "mucho" for "very" made his attempt sound clumsy. Rudolfo sprung on this clumsiness and let Miles know that using Spanish incorrectly wasn't acceptable at this moment. Rudolfo's insult pushed Miles to retaliate with a real mock Spanish statement, simply putting final "o" sounds onto English words. It was as if to say, "If I can't try to really speak Spanish, then I'll mock it to pieces." I heard Miles employ this mock technique on other occasions as well. I asked him about this use in our mid-year interview.

MILES: Yeah, I do that. I don't know. I just say some stuff like, *"Hello-o, come here-o."* Like the Spanish. They're like Mexicans, they're like, *"No hablo inglés"* {I don't speak English}. "Oh, you don't understand English? Okay. *"Come-o here-o now-o."* And then they're like, "Shut up!" It's just a— I don't know, I just say it.

DJANGO: Is it kinda clowning them?

MILES: Kinda, pretty much.

(January 19, 2007)

Miles described using this hyper-mock Spanish as retaliation. In his interaction with Rudolfo it was retaliation for feeling disrespected by Rudolfo for calling out his Spanish attempt. In this interview he spoke of retaliation against bilingual Latino/as who sometimes played as if they didn't understand English. In both cases Miles saw this as part of a larger genre of clowning and ritual insult using language and ethnicity as core game pieces in verbal battles.[20] Although such mock uses were not ratified as sharing across traditional lines, they were also not wholly negative within the genre of African American word play common across groups at South Vista.

Most Latino/a youth in general viewed African American and Pacific Islander sharing in Spanish as both complimentary and necessary. While ratification was a moment-to-moment affair, the overall sentiment was that uses of Spanish were a good and needed part of communication in South Vista. Carlos said this most thoroughly in our spring interview.

CARLOS: The one thing with the Black people – the African Americans here, and the Samoans, if you're Latino and you're talking to them then they try to talk in Spanish to you. Like if you give them something, like, "Let me have some soda," and then you give them soda, they're all like *"Gracias."* They just say something in Spanish.

DJANGO: What do you think about that?

C: They know some words. I think that's good, because that's like bringing our language, so they're doing it for us: They're bringing our language, that's a good thing. Because, I mean, Spanish is becoming famous here in the United States. It's needed at most places, especially because Latinos are migrating, and migrating.

(March 12, 2007)

Carlos saw that African Americans and Pacific Islanders tried at times to speak Spanish with him and his Latino/a peers. He even imagined a scenario. But it was his feelings about this sharing that were most important here. Although Carlos realized they only knew "some words," he still felt like his African American and Pacific Islander peers were "doing it for us," a complimentary vision of sharing Spanish. At the same time he also knew that these peers needed the Spanish language that was omnipresent in his changing community and was becoming ever more so across the nation. As Carlos said, "Latinos are migrating, and migrating."

In the face of this migration, a major desire to learn Spanish was born. It was a desire that pulled African American and Pacific Islander youth toward Spanish, even as the school and the dominant society beyond South Vista pushed them toward English. The force of this desire for learning coupled with peer networks of Spanish speakers and particular social purposes of flirting, insult, and cultural bridges made up an important system of small crossings and sharings into Spanish (see Table 2 for a summary of these processes). In my observations and conversations, male African American and Pacific Islander youth participated in these uses of Spanish more often than their female counterparts due to differing social networks. However, the desire to understand and use Spanish transcended gender and social networks. All Pacific Islander and African American youth I came to know at South Vista wanted to know Spanish.

Table 2. *Processes of Spanish crossing and sharing*

Process	Example
Desire & learning	I try to learn what they are saying – Rahul
Complimentary	That's our language, so they're doing it for us – Carlos
Necessary	Spanish is the second language of the US – Rahul
Unratified mock Spanish	Stop talking like that, you embarrass yourself – Rudy
Ratified mock Spanish	Hey, *¿Por qué, amigo?* You know, all that stuff – Rahul
Speech Acts	
Ritual insult	You don't got no *músculo* – Ela
Flirting	*¿Qué quieres?* – Miles
Cultural bridges	*¿Cómo estás?* – Miles

SHARING THE FUNDS OF KNOWLEDGE IN SCHOOLS

If we are going to make serious attempts at sharing cultural space in multiethnic classrooms and in a multiethnic society, then we must attend carefully to how Spanish and other languages participate in challenging and reinforcing ethnic division in positive and difficult ways. Understanding the ways Spanish works to solidify crucial ties to family and peers, to leave others frustrated and confused in multiethnic classrooms and, in small ways, to engender communication and relationship across ethnicity has become increasingly important in urban America, given the continuing segregation of communities of color and major demographic shifts in neighborhoods toward Latino/a majorities.

One major use of this understanding is to capitalize on the desire for Spanish by non-speakers for the educational and social benefit of all youth. It was certainly ironic that African American and Pacific Islander youth at South Vista, surrounded by

Spanish-speaking peers, were enrolled in Spanish classes with only one target language speaker; their Latina teacher. This one Spanish class was charged with fulfilling the desire to learn Spanish and all the youth in my work knew the class was not equipping them with the needed competence. In effect, they had real-life Spanish language tests daily in youth space. This is not a critique of their Spanish teacher. She was a qualified, caring, innovative teacher who students counted among their favorite teachers. Rather, it is our model of additional language education that needs rethinking, particularly when the stakes for language learning are as high as they are in many urban districts.

The resources for real language learning surrounded Ela, Miles, Rahul, Rochelle, and their peers. I thought more and more as the year progressed about what it would mean to share *funds of knowledge* (Moll, 1992; Moll and Gonzales, 1994) rather than using them only for the educational benefit of the group who brings those funds to school. The funds of knowledge concept forwarded by Luis Moll and his colleagues looks to use the cultural and linguistic knowledge young people use in their communities outside school as the foundation for academic learning inside the classroom. We have tended to view the utility of funds of knowledge and general-resource approaches to language and culture only as they apply to particular marginalized groups in relative isolation from each other. We have much educational research that brings Spanish language and the social work and learning expectations of particular Latino/a communities into classrooms serving Latino/a students. Language and literacy research has shown how it can be a powerful tool for exploring, honoring, and extending those linguistic and sociocultural practices.[21] But what about sharing these funds of linguistic and cultural knowledge with the other young people in the community who want and need to benefit from them?

At South Vista the beginnings of such sharing in Spanish was already underway, but school is an ideal position to formalize such pluralist tendencies for the benefit of all students. What Rahul called the "second language of the US" was needed in youth space, in the South Vista community, and in the larger society. A model of language education that began to use the linguistic skills and knowledge of Latino/as as resources not only for their own learning, but also for the learning of their African American and Pacific Islander peers was direly needed. Rather than one target speaker for language learning (the teacher), why not have several target speakers composed of peers? Such models of language education would work to benefit all youth as they could share their linguistic repertoires with each other, in effect working to sustain facility in their own ways with words and build up facility in the ways of others in their communities. Some dual immersion models, of course, follow this general program. Yet, at South Vista, like in the vast majority of multiethnic urban schools in the United States, students were completely isolated from their Spanish-speaking peers when they were being taught Spanish.

The lessons I learned at South Vista also go beyond language learning to offer new possibilities for understanding divisions and tensions between marginalized communities. Beneath the surface of communicative frustration and mistrust, the linguistic desire, crossing, and sharing of African American and Pacific Islander students provides excellent material for lessons on interethnic respect and understanding. Add this to the fact that many Latino/a and Pacific Islander youth participated heavily in African American Language and Hip Hop culture and it becomes clear that interethnic linguistic and cultural sharing holds important keys for bringing youth together to respect each other's contributions to multiethnic youth space and to our multiethnic society. In addition to language learning, then, classroom discussions of linguistic and cultural sharing should be at the heart of learning about the way pluralism is enacted by both maintaining and sharing cultural practices. In the United States, this learning could work to break through long-standing tensions between African American and Latino/a youth in particular. These pedagogical and curricular suggestions bring us into the terrain of a *pedagogy of pluralism* – a stance to teaching within and across difference in multiethnic educational contexts. I will outline additional practical aspects of this pedagogical stance at the conclusion of each chapter in this book. If we are going to make serious attempts at sharing cultural space in multiethnic classrooms and in a multiethnic society, then we must attend carefully to the paradox of pluralism at the heart of these tensions. "It's our culture, we have to," said Carlos. "When I'm around Black people I try to speak English," Carlos also said. Carlos and his African American and Pacific Islander peers were poised to push further to understand the role of Spanish in their youth community. As educators and humanizing social language researchers we must find the poise to join them; pushing further ourselves to use such understandings to foster respect and relationship within and across difference.

3 "True Samoan": ethnic solidarity and linguistic reality

It was February 7th, 2007, and basketball season was coming to a close. I had been practicing with the girls and boys several times a week since October and had attended many of their home and away games.[1] The girls had just finished their practice and the boys were running a full court scrimmage. Ela, her cousin Soa, and I sat on the scorer's table beside the court, still in our basketball clothes. We watched the boys sprint from end to end, listening to their constant trash-talking and making comments about their play. There was some lament in the air. The two young women mentioned how sad they were that basketball season was almost over. They looked dejected and I felt the same. It was a sadness I remembered from my own high-school seasons. Daily practices and weekly games, the camaraderie, having a common goal and focus with your peers, having something to look forward to all day during class. Then something happened that brought us out of our morose: Ela said something quickly to Soa in Samoan. I had heard very few exchanges between Samoan speakers over my year; this was somewhat remarkable.

"You gotta teach me some Samoan one of these days," I said.

Ela suddenly beamed, a spark in her eye. "Right now!" she demanded, "Soa, get the paper and the pen!"

We sat on the scorer's table, the boys practicing in front of us: Ela writing down and pronouncing words and phrases in Samoan, me attempting to pronounce them in all their multi-stressed grandeur. Ela laughed at me when I struggled, and nodded in surprise when I came close in pronunciation. A few minutes in and our list was ten deep. Ela paused to think. "What else?" she said. I asked her the phrase for "come here" {sau'ii} and the phrase for "go away" {alu ese}.

The boys were taking a water break and Soa was across the court practicing her three-point shot. "Sau'ii!" I called. Soa smiled and came over. I turned on her in the mock anger that was a common game among the players. "Alu ese!" I demanded. She and Ela cracked up.

"You hella mean!" Soa said as she laughed her way back onto the court.

During the next thirty minutes, Ela wrote down an extensive list of words and phrases. She taught me how to say "beautiful" {aulelei}, "fuck off" {ufa ese!}, "Hello, how are you?" {Talofa o ai lou igoa?}, and the personal pronouns "I" {au}, "you" {oe}, "we" {tatou}, and "they" {latou}. She told me how to say, "I love you" {E alofa au la oe} and encouraged me to say it to Rae when I got home that night (which I, of course, did). With "I love you," I even got a rudimentary introduction to Samoan syntax as she made a translation diagram of the sentence for me like this:

I love   you
↓   ↓   ↓
Au alofa oe

I love you
E alofa au la oe

She sent me off that day with the sheet and told me to practice (she checked up on me in the days and weeks following our lesson). Ela and I had had a lot of fun to this point in the year. I had learned many incredible and difficult things about her life. Other than on the basketball court, I had never shared an activity with her where we were both so fully engaged. Here is a reproduction of the sheet Ela wrote for me that February day.

Hello, how are you?	I play basketball
Talofa o ai lou igoa?	E taalo au basketball
My name is Django	Bring my money
O lo'u igoa o Django	aumai lou kupe

Where you from?	Church
O fea e te sau ai?	Loku
Where you born?	Friends
O fea le mea na e fanau ai?	U'o
Shut up	I = au
Mapugi lou gutu	You = oe
	We=tatou
Fuck off	They= latou
Ufa ese	
Come here	Hey!
Sau'ii	Sole!
Go away	Ugly
Alu ese	Auleaga
	Beautiful
	Aulelei

I begin this section with a vignette of Samoan youth Ela and Soa, and me to illuminate the cherished cultural practice of Pacific Islander languages that *were* easy to miss in the multiethnic youth space of South Vista. In fact, it was four months before I witnessed the exchange that led to Ela's impromptu language lesson. Sure, I had spoken at length with Ela, Rahul, and other Pacific Islanders about their heritage languages, but I had witnessed little talk in youth space. This is not to say that such talk did not happen, but it was not highly visible at South Vista, a point that I will support from Latino/a and African American youth perspectives as well. In effect, the spaces for Samoan, Tongan, Fijian, and Hindi[2] use were far more limited than those for Spanish. Spanish, of course, had vast numbers of speakers and interlocutors and was in some respects supported by the school language offerings and by the many Spanish/English bilingual teachers. The fact that a marginalized language does not have many speakers at a school, however, does not buy educators out of the responsibility to acknowledge and respond to it. Nor does it free youth peers from the need to negotiate such deeply marginalized languages as sites of difference and division.

In this chapter I explore the processes of solidarity, exclusion, and maintenance of Pacific Islander languages at South Vista. I seek an analysis that will illuminate the ways linguistic and ethnic solidarity interacted with linguistic reality. That is, I am interested in understanding the intersection of linguistic identity and the constraints of youth community languages with very few speakers. It is worth noting at the outset that little research (language and literacy focused or otherwise) has looked into the schooling experiences of Polynesian youth in particular or Pacific Islander youth more broadly even though they are a significant population in the major cities of the western United States.[3] Work is sorely needed by researchers conversant in the cultures and languages of the Pacific Islands, particularly the Polynesian Islands. Although I do not possess those proficiencies, I am hopeful that my work can begin this inquiry and add to our knowledge of school and other institutional experiences for those truly isolated from their heritage languages and cultural ways of being.

"BARELY": LATINO/A AND AFRICAN AMERICAN PERSPECTIVES ON PACIFIC ISLANDER LANGUAGES

In addition to thinking generally about the ways Pacific Islander languages reinforced and challenged notions of difference and division in multiethnic youth space, another question echoed through my thinking about the heritage languages of Ela, Rahul, Soa, and their Pacific Islander peers. What happens to languages in youth space when there are few people to speak them and few people who will understand? One answer to this question is rather simple; they don't get used much. The lack of noticeable presence was one major response I received from African American and Latino/a youth when we talked about Pacific Islander languages. In fact, in contrast to the prevalence of solicited and unsolicited content about Spanish and AAL in my student interviews across ethnic groups, I usually had to

explicitly ask African American and Latino/a youth for their thinking about Pacific Islander languages. It was not a topic that dominated their everyday consciousness in the ways Spanish and AAL
use did and so required me to ask more directly. Take this response
from Carlos about the languages of his Pacific Islander peers.

> DJANGO: What about their languages, like Fijian, or Tongan, or
> Samoan? Do you hear it ever?
> CARLOS: Barely. Samoan, I mean, between them, like when
> they're talking to each other I hear. But other than that, no.
> (March 12, 2007)

When asked directly Carlos reflected on the fact that he "barely"
heard these languages. Although he did recall hearing Samoan
spoken between Pacific Islander youth, he noted this was not a regular occurrence. The fact that he singles out Samoan is also significant.
I found that in the sense-making of Latino/a and African American
youth, the names of Pacific Islander languages were often indiscrim-
inately interchanged. Carlos may have meant Samoan here, though
he had no Samoan speakers in his peer groups or classes. He did,
however, have Fijian and Hindi speakers in his classes. He may also
have been using "Samoan" to speak generally about Pacific Islander
languages as other youth often used "Tongan" or "Samoan" to mean
any of these languages.

When I asked Miles directly about the languages he heard less
often among his peers, he echoed Carlos's feeling that they were
barely heard.

> DJANGO: There are also other languages at the school that you
> don't hear as much. Like what other languages?
> MILES: Tongan and Samoan. You hear Soa and Ela speak a tiny
> bit.
> D: A little bit?
> M: But not really.
> (March 26, 2007)

Like Carlos, Miles only heard these languages very occasionally. This is quite significant as Ela and Soa were part of Miles' peer group, played basketball with him daily for several months, and were in many of his classes. The fact that he only heard Ela and Soa use their Samoan "a tiny bit" and "not really" given their shared social network at school was important. Also important was the way "Samoan" and "Tongan" got conflated for Miles as they did for Carlos. For Miles, Soa and Ela might have spoken either. This lack of consciousness about these languages led to a lack of prestige among youth that followed in the general ethnic geography mapped out by Latino/a and African American youth at South Vista. Although my interview and fieldnote data with Black and Latino/a youth is full of comments, conversations, and sense-making about race and ethnicity at South Vista, the vast majority is centered on Latino/as and African Americans. Pacific Islanders, marginalized in number and heritage language, were also often marginalized in who counted as a major player in the sorts of divisions drawn through multiethnic youth space.

It should not be surprising, then, that I did not document the sorts of exclusion and frustration around these languages that dominated African American and Pacific Islander perspectives on Spanish use. In fact, in over 400 hours of observations inside and outside the classrooms of South Vista High, I only witnessed one concrete, albeit brief, example comparable to exclusion and solidarity that were commonplace through Spanish use. I recorded the interaction in my fieldnotes on October 16th, 2006, between three Fijian Indian students, Ramesh, Chitra, and Sheeba, and an African American young man named Chris.

> After school in the front walkway I see Ramesh again with Chitra and Sheeba. Ramesh nods his head at one of them and says, "Bolla!"
> He looks at me and says, "That's Fijian. It means, 'what's up?' "
> He then looks over at his friend Chris standing a few feet away and says loudly, "Bolla!"

Chris looks at Ramesh shaking his head and says, "I don't
know what you're saying."
Ramesh looks back at me and says, "See, they have no idea
what we're saying."

Ramesh was clearly putting on a bit of a show for me. He knew I
was interested in language and went out of his way to translate
then show how he could exclude others through language. Even
if the exclusion was done for my benefit, though, it did show the
rarely realized possibility of exclusion through Pacific Islander
languages.

To be clear, I am not arguing that exclusion through Pacific
Islander languages did not happen in the youth space of South Vista.
Rather, I am attempting to illustrate how infrequent it was in comparison to exclusion through Spanish. In fact, Carla, Rosa, and
Miles could not think of times this happened when asked directly.
However, exclusion did happen, as Julio and Carlos mentioned in
separate interviews. In our interview on March 12th, 2007, Carlos
attempted to level the linguistic exclusion of Spanish with that of
Hindi and other Pacific Islander languages at South Vista. In doing
so, he revealed a perspective on in-group language use akin to Miles'
assessment about Spanish; that all ethnic groups would exclude if
they could.

CARLOS: And I think everybody does [exclude through language].
Well, African Americans, they obviously can't do it 'cause they
only speak English. But the Pacific Islanders, they do it too.
DJANGO: Sometimes they'll just speak in their language a bit? So
you've heard Samoan or Tongan or Fijian around here before?
You've heard them talking?
C: Yeah, the Fijians do it a lot in class. 'Cause they're like stuck
to each other a lot. They're like – 'cause there's a little bit of
them, so they stick together and in class that's all they speak,
like to each other. And sometimes when we're like doing math
problems or like questions and stuff and they're doing that,

we're all like, "Okay, speak English. We want to know." But
then I think about how we do that too.

D: Right, that's kind of how it works.

C: I'm just like – it's fair.

This did not happen in many social or academic spaces for Carlos. He could only think of his math class as an example. Yet when it did happen it was cause for reflection on his personal habits of solidarity and exclusion. "We do that too" was a way for Carlos to say that it was an ordinary in-group move to exclude through language, whether for working out a math problem or for making a joke between friends. Here, Carlos went so far as to call such moments of solidarity and exclusion "fair."

At the same time, Carlos and his peers saw that the linguistic playing field was hardly level. The fact that there were just a few Fijian Indians speaking Hindi made it easier to dismiss such moments as fair rather than as linguistically frustrating or cause for mistrust. I will provide further evidence of this lack of frustration and ease from Julio. Before leaving Carlos's take, though, I want to emphasize his comment about African Americans. Carlos, like Miles in his discussion of Spanish exclusion, mentioned that the only group at the school that could not engage in this sort of complete linguistic exclusion was African Americans. Although I remain focused here on Pacific Islanders and their heritage languages, such understandings continue to build toward a fuller exploration of the role of AAL in South Vista which I take up in Chapter 4.

A final perspective from Julio reinforced the notion that Pacific Islander languages were not a major site of contestation or division for Latino/a and African American students at South Vista. In our January interview, we had spoken at length about Spanish use and perceptions when I finally asked Julio directly about other languages.

DJANGO: So obviously Spanish is spoken at the school a lot. Any other languages you ever hear here?

JULIO: I heard Tongan. I heard three Indians were talking, talking like their Indian language, but those don't really bother me.

D: But it's kind of just a little bit here and there or whatever?

J: Yeah.

D: Not in the classes?

J: I mean between them they probably talk like a whole soap opera about everything. I don't really care.

(January 16, 2007)

Julio, like others, mentioned only a time or two he heard these languages over my year of talking with him. Most striking here is Julio's lack of frustration over being excluded by the "Indian" (Fijian Indian) students he recalled. Beyond a lack of frustration was a lack of concern, typified by the statement "I don't really care." The fact is that Julio and his peers didn't have to care. Recall that most youth didn't even mention times of use or exclusion through Pacific Islander languages. Whereas Spanish was omnipresent in the multiethnic youth space of South Vista, these languages were barely present. Julio imagined that "between them they probably talk a whole soap opera." Yet this was speculated. Pacific Islander, African American, and Latino/a youth did not have to speculate about the prevalence of Spanish. They did not have to imagine long stretches of talk and social interaction where divisions, solidarities, and exclusions were enacted through Spanish language. The situation with Pacific Islander languages was quite different. Simply put, Latino/a and Black youth were not forced to care much about the few speakers on the margins of youth space that talked Samoan, Tongan, Fijian, or Hindi amongst themselves.

The understandings of the Latino/a and African American youth in my work coupled with the rare observations I made of Pacific Islander languages used as a tool of in-group solidarity and out-group exclusion begin to illustrate how these languages did not hold the presence, prestige, or power of Spanish to divide and exclude at South

Vista. But what about the speakers of these languages? Did they treasure these languages in the ways Latino/as treasured Spanish? And what role did the heritage languages of these youth play in their identities as Samoans, Tongans, Fijians, or Fijian Indians? The afternoon I spent with Ela and Soa in the gym learning some rudimentary Samoan, the spark in Ela's eye that day, and those intense moments of engagement pushes me to reckon with these questions even as I write. And it pushed me throughout the school year to reckon with the reasons these languages were so silenced in youth space, and where and how they found voice beyond it.

ELA AND HER LANGUAGE

In the following analysis, I use the experiences and perspectives of Ela as a window into these questions. Ela, born and raised in American Samoa, came to the United States and South Vista to join her grandparents, aunt, and cousins just three years before I met her. I also call some on Rahul in this section to add to the understandings mapped out by Ela. Rahul, born and raised in South Vista, grew up with predominantly Hindi-speaking parents who were both born and raised in Fiji. These two youth had different relationships to their heritage languages and to homelands far off in the Pacific Ocean that I believe provide evidence for understanding the processes of language solidarity, maintenance, and choice at play in their lives and those of their Pacific Islander peers.

Samoan linguistic and ethnic identity simmered below the surface of multiethnic youth space for Ela. She did not use her Samoan often at school, a point her friend Miles made for me earlier in this chapter. And yet Ela's connection to her heritage language and culture was as intense as any of the youth I met at South Vista. She fought fiercely to voice her Samoaness even as so much of it was drowned out by the sheer numbers and the local and national histories of Latino/as and African Americans. Sometimes Ela's struggle to voice her ethnic identity simmered over into school space, as it did in the following interaction.

On a very warm March day I sat out on a bench in front of the school as lunch was ending. Ela, Soa, and their male Samoan friend, Tua, spent most of their free time together with a few other Samoans. They were also often joined by Rochelle, or Miles, or a number of other African American youth that made up weaker ties in their school social network. Even if they were among themselves, it was usually within earshot of non-Samoan students. So it was not unusual to see them hanging together, but as I sat and watched them from the bench that day most of the students had already made the slow march toward class. It was a rare moment with just the three of them in their own fleeting youth space. Ela stood in the front driveway, in front of the main entrance, in the most public place in the school. She looked at Tua and Soa, flexed her muscles in the mock pose of a body builder and yelled "Hamos!!!" (Samoan!!!) All three of them busted up laughing (as did I when they looked over). For just a moment Ela had shown herself, had flexed her Samoaness for her peers. Then we all headed toward class where such exhibitions of these particular selves were highly unlikely to occur.

There were other times I glimpsed fragments of this Samoaness which remained silenced or hidden in youth space. In a January interview with Ela she opened up her backpack to reveal a sarong, a modern approximation of a traditional wrap worn by men and women in important ceremonies back in Samoa. I asked her why she had it in her backpack and she told me that she needed to wear it in church that afternoon. What I, many of her Latino/a and African American peers, and her teachers did not see was that Ela and Soa often had these sarongs stuffed in their backpacks, waiting for another cultural space far from school for expression; waiting for church. In fact, according to Ela and her Samoan peers, in addition to the home, South Vista's Samoan church was the major location of Samoan language use, learning, and maintenance in the community.[4]

Let me provide a snapshot of True Message Samoan Baptist Church, the Christian church Ela and her Samoan community attended.[5] I believe this description will help me provide a clearer picture of the role churches and other community organizations play in addition to school for marginalized youth, communities, and languages with few numbers in multiethnic schools and cities. And because home and church were the major domains of Samoan language use, I believe it is important to look into a space of voice in addition to school and youth space which were spaces of relative silencing.

After many interviews and classroom observations, and after months of playing basketball together, Ela and I had developed significant trust. On several occasions I took her and Soa home from basketball practice or to church. In late February Ela invited Rae and me to her church for the service at "youth night." What follows is an excerpt from my fieldnotes of our visit on March 2nd, 2007.

Rae and I find a pew on the left side and a man in front of us (who later turns out to be a church leader) shakes our hands and welcomes us. It is very bright inside the church and there are no windows. Banners adorn the front wall exclaiming, "Christ is our savior" and "Alleluia!" There are three sections of pews about seven rows deep. A couple of small steps go up in the front to a sort of pulpit. Six large vases of artificial white orchids are placed on either side of the lectern. In the far right corner are the band and singers; a drum set, a piano, two keyboards, a bass, and five singers. Within 15 minutes the small church is pretty full with 35 young people from infants to teenagers and more than 20 adults.

The congregation begins singing. Junior, a student at the school, is singing and points at me and smiles. A large screen comes down behind the pulpit and the words to the songs in both Samoan and English scroll along. The first song is sung completely in English, then completely in Samoan, the second is the opposite. Rae and I tentatively sing along in English, then more hum and sing in Samoan.

After the songs end the priest, who is wearing a traditional red sarong and top, instructs us to go around and shake hands and greet our neighbors. Soa tells us to follow her and we go along, shaking hands with the children and adults, smiling and offering greetings.

Later, we are introduced to Ela and Soa's aunt, who is holding her baby. The aunt tells us her family just came over from Samoa. Soa then tells us she herself has been to the church on Fridays only a few times, but that she comes every Sunday. Soa says that Ela comes more often to practice with the choir.

The younger women, including Ela and Soa, are in typical urban wear with sarongs over their jeans. Some of the elder women and men wear only traditional wraps. The younger men are dressed in urban wear; baggie jeans, kicks, collared shirts and do not wear sarongs. The older members speak Samoan and English during a mock debate about Jesus and Satan, while the younger members speak mainly in English. Ela, however, speaks mainly Samoan in her group the entire time.

During the evening Soa and her aunt act as our interpreters, translating for us what is said in Samoan (and even sometimes explaining what is said in English).

I was struck by many things in our visit to True Message Church. Soa's kindness as she tirelessly translated for our benefit. Ela's beautiful singing voice as she belted out the gospel in Samoan. There were many practices present at the church that I never saw in the multiethnic youth space at the heart of my research. Seeing the cultural practices alive at True Message influenced my thinking about the role of Samoan and other Pacific Islander languages at South Vista High. Here was a space far from school where Ela and Soa wore their sarongs, where they heard and spoke and understood the Samoan language, where they read Samoan on the screen and in the Bible.[6] This, of course, is far oversimplified. Many of the children and teenagers were not speaking Samoan or wearing sarongs. They were, however, surrounded by these facets of Samoaness that were not at all a part of their school days.

I want to avoid a romanticization of this church space. I provide this description and comment not simply to bask in the possibility of linguistic and cultural maintenance under conditions of severe marginalization. Rather, I provide this snapshot as a contrast to what I and Latino/a and African American youth barely heard or saw in youth space. It is also important for me to mention that all the youth in my work attended churches and temples where their languages and cultures were celebrated and practiced, but for Pacific Islanders it was one of the only beyond-home spaces of this practice and celebration.

Over the year, Ela helped me make better sense of what I witnessed at True Message Church. As I talked with Ela in our interviews, I began to grasp the role the church played as a forum of linguistic and cultural learning and expression, as well as the complicated relationship between South Vista Pacific Islander youth and their heritage languages. I quote at length from a mid-year interview because Ela illuminated several key factors in the way Pacific Islander languages were hyper-marginalized in the youth space of South Vista.

> DJANGO: Does everybody speak Samoan in the church or do some people not?
>
> ELA: Like all the teenagers, their parents speak only Samoan, but they were born here. And when they speak Samoan, they just … (laughs and shakes her head). They don't even know how to pronounce the words.
>
> D: Okay, and so do you make fun of them or what?
>
> E: It's funny when they speak, when you're over here and they talk. They don't know how to speak Samoan … Only me and Soa, one of my cousins. She just came from Samoa. We're the only ones that like to speak Samoan – like true Samoan.
>
> D: And what does that mean to you, knowing how to speak Samoan?

E: It's good because you know our grandparents – they speak Samoan the whole time. They get mad at us when we speak English.

D: And so you have plans to maybe go back to Samoa, right? If you stayed here, and had a family here, would you want your kids to speak Samoan?

E: Both, if they speak Samoan [first].

D: Do they teach these teenagers in church how to speak?

E: Yeah ... one of our Sunday school teachers, they teach them how to speak Samoan, but they don't like to speak Samoan.

D: Really?

E: They don't like to speak it.

D: Oh, you mean the teenagers who were born here?

E: Uh-huh.

D: Okay, what do you think about that?

E: I can't believe their parents are Samoan, but they don't even know how to speak Samoan. They can't speak.

D: Do you consider them to be Samoan?

E: (*Laughs*) I don't choose – it's up to them.

D: No, but I mean like if someone has some parents that were born in Samoa, but they were born here and they can't speak it, are they as Samoan as you, or not?

E: Yeah.

D: You think they are.

E: They look like us, like, but when they speak ... (*shakes her head and smiles*).

(January 7, 2007)

Some of Ela's remarks echoed those of her bilingual Latino/a peers. They, too, were motivated by monolingual and Spanish-dominant elders to use and maintain their heritage language. Here and other times in informal and formal interviews, Ela reported her grandparents getting mad at her for speaking English with them. This fear of the older generations about losing Samoan required action beyond the home, though. There was no support at school and there were hardly the numbers of speakers to ensure young people would practice the language with each other. This is where the church came in. Church was a place where young people took Samoan language lessons, where they used a Bible written in Samoan, and where Samoan speaking was encouraged during services and events.

Even with the cultural space of church where young people were encouraged to go on Friday nights ("youth night") and Sundays, still Ela commented that they could not speak Samoan well. She felt this was especially true of youth who were born and raised in South Vista. Remember that time-in-country was an important factor in Spanish as a tool of solidarity and exclusion, too. Recall South Vista native Alberto who could not speak Spanish well enough for his Mexican-born Latina peers. To Ela, there were very few young people at the school and in the broader Samoan community who could speak "true Samoan." She and Soa were different because they had spent most of their lives in the home country before coming to South Vista. And Ela could not believe it was possible to have parents born in Samoa and not know how to speak the language. For Ela, who could speak and write in Samoan, this was unimaginable.[7] She would encourage her future children to speak both languages, but only if they spoke Samoan first (remember also that Julio had similar sentiments about Spanish).

There was a further layer to Ela's understanding of Samoan use among her peers, as she said, "They don't like to speak it." This statement spoke to the many factors working together to silence Pacific Islander languages at South Vista. One major factor, of course, was lack of numbers. Another was the lack of proficiency of many Pacific Islander youth, which Ela spoke to in our interview. Working together with these forces to create a linguistic reality of relative silence in youth space was a fierce competition with AAL and youth culture for the hearts and voices of Pacific Islander youth. That is, many Pacific Islander youth who had been in the United States and South Vista most or all of their lives chose to speak English, and AAL in particular, when they were outside their homes and churches.[8] This lies in stark contrast to the relative lack of such clear-cut choices for Latino/as, who, like Alberto, understood Spanish as a vital tool of solidarity and ethnic identity in youth space regardless of his time-in-country and relative proficiency in that language. This is not to say that many bilingual Latino/a youth did not sometimes choose the very same AAL, but that in my observations they did not choose Englishes over Spanishes as a rule in youth space.

Even given this tension over language choice and proficiency, Ela still regarded the youth who couldn't speak Samoan and didn't like to as legitimately Samoan. It was up to them to choose their ethnic identity. In fact, Ela made a complex move here, showing the twin identity prerequisites of language and phenotype. While language was a primary marker of identity, you also had to look the part; "They look like us, but when they speak ..." and she shook her head in the negative and smiled. Although Ela herself was amazed at the possibility of being Samoan without proficiency in the language, she recognized that what you look like is also a major factor.[9] She was also, perhaps, coming to terms with what Samoaness meant in South Vista; what it meant for the first generation youth there and, possibly, what it would mean for the future years of her community.

During most of the year of my study Ela was set on returning to Samoa after high school to live her adult life there. While she realized being a Samoan youth in South Vista did not necessarily include fluency in Samoan, she also was cautious about what the language meant back home. She related this in a later interview.

> ELA: My grandma said now in Samoan if you don't speak
> Samoan good, you can't have a job ... Because a lot of kids from
> Samoa came over here and they went back and they didn't even
> know how to speak Samoan. I was like, "What?"
> DJANGO: And you can write it, too, huh?

E: I can speak, I can write, because my grandma *be talking* – my grandma, she *be talking* Samoan to me.

(March 5, 2008)

Ela was explicit here about the requirements of her homeland and, again, about the role of her grandparents in keeping her prepared to be Samoan in Samoa, not just in South Vista. The dual forces of connection to homeland and communication with elders kept Ela, like her Mexican-born peers Carla and Julio, determined and concerned about maintaining her heritage language. Yet for Pacific Islander youth, their lack of numbers and speakers in youth space and in the community made these forces somewhat more dramatic. That is, there were major tensions eating at these connections for Ela and her Pacific Islander peers that were also present for Latino/a youth, but were tempered for Latino/as by the omnipresence of Spanish and sheer numbers of Spanish speakers.

Linguistically, one of the main actors in this tension was evident even in the grammar of Ela's final comment, "She *be talking* Samoan to me" (for a rough DAE translation, "She is usually or always talking Samoan"). Ela, herself a relatively recent member of the South Vista youth speech community, was here already participating in AAL grammar.[10] Chapter 4 will center on the meaning of AAL crossing and sharing practices for notions of difference, division, and unity in multiethnic schools and communities.

The True Message Church and other churches certainly played an important role in the cultural and linguistic landscape of Pacific Islanders at South Vista. Yet, as the year wore on, I began to think more about the dislike of speaking Samoan Ela mentioned and its relationship to the pull of youth culture and AAL. Soa, for instance, began to resist going to church in the final months of my study. Ela became less sure she would return to Samoa. In the year following my study, Ela was on and off with her participation in choir and talked about being interested in singing in a Hip Hop group instead. Even during the year the powerful currents of church, elders, and

homeland that pulled Ela away from the more highly locally prestigious practices of AAL and youth culture seemed to be waning.[11]

Battling in the throes of the paradox of pluralism, Ela and
many of her peers struggled to maintain consistent ethnic solidarity through oral language in youth space, even as they were pulled
to cross into shared linguistic practices with other groups. This was
even truer for Pacific Islanders like Rahul, who were born and raised
in South Vista. Rahul, who spoke primarily Hindi with his Fijian
Indian parents, never did so in the multiethnic youth space of South
Vista. Rahul took a rather pragmatic, if somewhat painful view of his
linguistic reality. As we sat alone in the gym in December, Rahul
explained why he didn't use his Hindi at school.

> DJANGO: You told me last time that Hindi's not really something
> that you've spoken at school before too much.
> RAHUL: No, I don't really speak my Hindi.
> D: Tell me more about that?
> R: Well, it's not that I'm ashamed about it, I'm glad I speak
> Hindi. But it's like there's no one to talk to in Hindi. If I know
> English, I'm gonna talk in English, you know? And Hindi's
> like – I would probably speak Hindi if it was another Fijian
> person and for a time I could talk about something here, which
> is like never, though. So that's it. I don't get a chance to speak
> my own language. Even if I want to, I wouldn't get a chance. I
> can't speak to myself, like, "Oh, yeah, you wanna talk Hindi,
> too?" "What the fuck is he doing? Talking to himself?" "Is he
> mumbling?"
>
> (December 8, 2006)

Rahul was clear to say here and on other occasions that he was not
ashamed of his language. Instead, he saw the linguistic reality of few
interlocutors and his own multilingualism. Although there were
a handful of Fijian Indian Hindi speakers that Rahul could have
spoken with, they were not members of his multiethnic, Hip Hopper
peer group. Outside of those few possibilities, Rahul felt isolated. He

felt like he could not use his language as a tool of solidarity in youth space even if he wanted to. There was some sadness and frustration in Rahul's comments. It was, after all, "his own language," a treasured facet of ethnic identity, but he did not "get a chance" to use it. Instead he was left to imagine the ridicule of his peers if he spoke to himself in Hindi.

Rahul, like Ela, did have some outside school spaces to practice Hindi. Other than the home and visits to temple, there was a significant Fijian Indian population in the larger Metro Area. Rae and I witnessed this larger community when Rahul invited us to "Fiji Day," an annual event bringing several hundred Fijians together for cultural celebration. Like Ela and other Pacific Islanders, though, Rahul's heritage language was by and large silenced in multiethnic youth space. This did not mean that these youth did not find other powerful ways to index their ethnic and linguistic identities as Samoans, Fijians, or Tongans inside youth space. In Chapter 5 I provide analysis of the many sorts of texts these youth wrote and performed to draw lines of difference and to index in-group solidarity. However, oral heritage language, a major factor in these youth's identities and family communication, was not the same sort of player as other languages in reinforcing and challenging lines of division in youth space. This stood in major contrast to Spanish, which was a massive force in drawing such divisions through solidarity and exclusion.

Learning from Ela and Rahul and observing them and their Pacific Islander peers led me to a tentative understanding of factors at play in use and maintenance outside youth space and relative silencing within youth space. Table 3 represents this understanding.

HYPER-MARGINALIZED LANGUAGES IN SCHOOLS
The ethnic and linguistic makeup of South Vista made Spanish a major player in processes of solidarity and exclusion in multiethnic youth space. It was clear from a year of observing and talking to young people across groups that Spanish use was a factor in Latino/a ethnic

Table 3. *Factors in Pacific Islander language use and silencing*

Use outside youth space	
Demands of elders	*Our grandparents, they get mad at us when we speak English – Ela*
Connection to homeland	*If you don't speak Samoan good, you can't have a job – Ela*
Churches and temples	*They teach them how to speak Samoan – Ela*
Silencing inside youth space	
Lack of interlocutors	*There's no one to talk to in Hindi – Rahul*
Lack of proficiency	*They don't even know how to pronounce the words – Ela*
Choosing of AAL and youth language	*We talk ghetto a lot – Ela*

identity and in African American and Pacific Islander social frustration. The fact that the school mainly ignored the ways that Spanish worked to exclude inside and outside classrooms was remarkable and disturbing. It is a rather easy argument to call for educational remedies that will help youth understand the processes at work in Spanish use when it is so deeply a part of all of their social worlds.

But what do we do with the more intensely marginalized heritage languages? Pacific Islander languages did not have the numbers or the steady stream of immigration to ensure their healthy survival. Nor did they have the support of the school through classes or bilingual teachers. This is not to say the state of US bilingual education in Spanish is in any regard rosy[12] – we have many, many mountains to climb there, too, but Spanish is at least a major part of the educational dialogue. I wondered during my research, and I continue to wonder as I remain in contact with Ela, whether Samoan and other Pacific Islander languages are on their way to a slow local death at South Vista. In work on language death, maintenance, and shift, researchers have pointed to a lack of functional use, a lack of community domains for use, a lack of support by schools, and the power of dominant and popular languages over the market and over the minds of youth as factors in diminishing languages among such hyper-marginalized speakers.[13] All of these things are certainly true for Pacific Islander languages in South Vista.

In thinking about the present and future of Ela's Samoan language and those of her Pacific Islander peers at South Vista, I am reminded of the old playground saying that is used to quickly solve disputes over the rules of the game. "Majority rules!" shout some children, and the minority has to play along or leave. Sometimes the local politics of language feels this way, and it certainly did in the youth space and school space of South Vista. But just because a language has few speakers and an ethnicity has few members does not buy educators out of the need to be culturally and linguistically relevant to these students. To apply the rules we know about resource approaches to language and literacy learning only to the majority in our urban schools is unacceptable. We must embrace the practices of hyper-marginalized students and look to contrast and join them with school practices just as we attempt to do so for our African American and Latino/a students. This will take much more research than I provide in this study, but I hope my work is a start in this regard.

Moving just a little further into the practical realm of the pedagogy of pluralism, what could these languages bring to all students in the multiethnic classrooms of South Vista? Imagine the lessons about language structure and phonology that could emerge for all students if these languages were invited into the mix in genuine and honorable ways. Ela, Rahul, and so many of their Pacific Islander peers had major facets of self silenced in youth space and classroom space. Yet those selves, those riches, were waiting beneath the surface for invitations, for domains of use, for questions and problems to be posed. Such questions and *problem posing*,[14] I believe, would help both the speakers of those languages in their own academic and ethnic identity struggles and those, like teachers and students, who often forget that these languages are spoken by their students and their friends. I believe we are contributing to the atrophy of the linguistic and cultural dexterity of these youth, and so are contributing to shrinking the resources of students and communities. Ultimately, it's like Ela said, "they choose." As it stands, however, hyper-marginalized youth like Samoans and Fijians have to choose without all the choices put out clearly and equally before them. And in that case, the dominant ways are sure to win – and win completely.

SOLIDARITY AND EXCLUSION: ONLY HALF THE PARADOX

Chapters 2 and 3 have largely focused on the ways South Vista youth used oral language to index solidarity within their ethnic groups and to sometimes, purposefully and inadvertently, exclude those outside their ethnic group. This was the territory of the "separations" between ethnic groups that Julio spoke of in the prologue to the chapters. Spanish was the major linguistic player in these separations, in reinforcing traditional notions of difference and division by ethnicity. On a much lesser scale, Pacific Islander languages sometimes drew lines of division in multiethnic youth space, though this was hardly as contested or widespread. At face value these linguistic and ethnic separations may seem wholly negative. Yet as youth told me and showed me over my year of study with them, the negative was deeply joined with the positive. While Spanish use pushed some out, it also allowed a Latino/a community living within the larger dominant White, DAE-speaking society a safe space to foster self and community.[15] They battled within the larger school and DAE-speaking society to maintain the connection to the Spanish language, and practicing it in youth space was a significant act of daily linguistic agency in the face of marginalization. For many Black and Pacific Islander youth, though, this Spanish use often meant frustration or, in some cases, mistrust.

Such is the paradox of pluralism. In order to be a plural cultural space there must be many cultures and practices present. In order for those practices to be maintained, they must be used with other members who can use them. That use necessarily leaves others with different cultural repertoires out of the conversation. The struggle of exclusion and of silencing are certainly within the power of schools to address far more ably than they currently do. A start would be to include such topics in classroom dialogue, something I did not witness or hear about at South Vista. A further step would be to include such topics in a critical language awareness curriculum. I will return for a more thorough discussion of such a curriculum in the Interlude at the conclusion of Chapter 4. For now, I remain focused on the ways language, in particular Spanish, worked to provide solace for its native speakers while simultaneously locking out non-speakers.

Yet in-group solidarity and exclusion through Spanish and Pacific Islander languages only explains half of the paradox of pluralism. The other half of being in pluralist cultural space is sharing practices across groups that allow the space to remain united in the face of disparate repertoires. Remember Miles, "We all gotta stay together." While South Vista's multiethnic space demanded the maintenance of difference, it also demanded the forging of linguistic and cultural identities that created unity across such differences, which forged strength in the face of mutual marginalizations. It demanded the development of linguistic dexterity to communicate successfully and linguistic plurality to know how to. Although we can learn much about what it means to live in a pluralist society from what groups do to affirm their particular cultural ways of being in the face of marginalization, we can also learn much from what they do to reach across those ways into shared spaces of being. Both are demanded in a truly multiethnic and multilingual society. And both were present in the youth space of South Vista.

The desire for and small but important crossings and sharings in Spanish were one major occasion of such language reaching across difference. In effect, the ways African American and Pacific

Islander youth thought about and participated in Spanish was a way for them to work against the frustration and mistrust. It was a means for them to exercise linguistic agency by joining their Latino/a peers in communicative practices so dear to the majority of the South Vista community. Although crucial to the ways difference and division were enacted at South Vista, these crossings and sharings in Spanish were not the most significant space of language sharing. It was through deep participation in the grammar, lexicon and rhetorical traditions of African American Language that many Latino/a and Pacific Islander students joined their Black peers in most deeply redrawing notions of difference and division. It was through this sharing in AAL that South Vista youth forged the most sustained spaces of interethnic unity and, in doing so, invited educational and social language theory, research, and practice to learn from such cultural re-visioning.

4 "They're in my culture, they speak the same way": sharing African American Language at South Vista

African American Language (AAL), like Spanish, was impossible to miss as I spent time inside and outside the classrooms of South Vista. AAL is probably the most studied variety of English in the world, with over forty years of sociolinguistic scholarship investigating when, how, where, with whom, and why AAL has been and continues to be spoken by many African Americans.[1] These decades of scholarship have given us a rich understanding of the grammar, phonology, lexicon, systematicity, and rhetorical traditions of AAL.

The prevalence of AAL at South Vista was somewhat surprising given the relatively small number of African American students at the school and the relatively small number of African American residents of the city. Remember, though, that South Vista had been undergoing a dramatic demographic shift over the previous two decades. What was a predominantly Black city as late as 1990 had become a city with a major Spanish-speaking Latino/a majority during the 1990s. In 2006–07 only 17 percent of the students at South Vista High were African American. So why and how the prevalence of AAL in the talk of youth space? Who was speaking AAL, with whom, and for what purposes? Although the answers to these questions will take some time to explore, what I came to understand was that AAL was shared by many youth speakers across lines of ethnicity, pushing against traditional understandings of linguistic and ethnic division and, like other heritage languages at South Vista, AAL was creating spaces and educational possibilities for language and literacy learning across difference.

AAL GRAMMAR, LEXICON, AND RITUAL INSULT
AMONG BLACK YOUTH

All of the African American students I came to know at South Vista were speakers of AAL and DAE: their everyday speech both inside and outside the classroom showed major features associated with Black language, but they could also shift, to varying extents, into more dominant varieties of English. The fact that many African Americans can and do systematically use features of AAL in their everyday speech is a common understanding in the research literature.[2] Miles said this most succinctly as we sat on a bench near the athletic field informally talking on June 6th, 2007. "Every Black person is bilingual," he told me, "You gotta be because I was taught that it's harder for us and you have to use their language to get by. It's not an excuse, it's just the way it is. Black people can talk nigga or they can talk normal."

Miles understood there were communicative demands made on him and his African American community to know some DAE and to know AAL. And he saw this as a certain type of bilingualism, as distinct systems of communication he was responsible for. On the one hand was the dominant English, what he and his peers across groups had come to call "normal," "standard," or "perfect." As I will explore through the examples that follow, Miles and his peers had internalized the sociolinguistic fallacy that DAE was somehow perfect and normal, with AAL being "slang" and "ghetto," being less than normal and less than perfect even though they treasured AAL in many ways. Miles here called AAL "nigga," a term whose complex use and meaning in multiethnic youth space I devote an extensive section to in this chapter. For now, let it suffice to say that from multiple conversations with Miles about his understanding of the N-words what he meant here by "nigga" was probably close to "everyday between peers."[3] Had he pronounced this N-word with a fully realized final "r," this statement would have had entirely different semantics.

Given that Miles and his peers generally understood that African Americans in South Vista had a distinct way with language, it was not surprising that my fieldnotes, formal interviews, and recordings of informal conversations with Black youth were laden with lexical, grammatical, and phonological features of AAL, as well as larger rhetorical traditions of AAL. I will provide just a few brief examples here to give some voice to the prevalence of AAL use among South Vista's African American youth. I will follow these examples with Latino/a and Pacific Islander youth engaging in the same structures, words, and rhetorical traditions as their African American peers.

Grammar

I begin my analysis by recalling one afternoon when I was talking with Anthony, an African American young man on the basketball team, as we headed over to the gym for practice. I had been playing basketball with the boys' and girls' teams for two months by this point and Anthony called me coach as we strolled toward the gym. When I told him that he could call me Django, Anthony replied, "But you ø like a second coach to me" (February 15, 2006). In our exchange Anthony omitted the copula "to be" in "you ø like" instead of the DAE "You *are* like." Basically, the option of omitting the copula "to be", a major feature of AAL grammar, is available to speakers when using the present tense of "is" and "are."[4]

Other major features of AAL grammar were commonplace among the African American youth I came to know. In a conversation I had with another young man on the team, Terrell, about a bootleg CD he was purchasing from a friend, he explained, "He *BIN* had it, he ø just waitin for me to have the money" (May 8, 2007). In addition to a copula omission ("he ø just"), Terrell used the remote verbal marker *stressed been* in "He *BIN* had" to denote the fact that his friend had possessed the CD for some time and still had it. Part of a complex tense (when an action occurs) and aspect (how an action occurs) system of AAL, this feature is one of many that highlight the way AAL semantics can differ significantly from DAE.

My *ethnolinguistic*[5] interviews with Miles and Rochelle were also full of AAL features. In one interview, Rochelle made the statement, "*When people call me out my name,* I don't really *be* listening" (December 4, 2006). Here, Rochelle used a hallmark of AAL grammar known as the *habitual be* in "I don't really *be* listening" for the rough DAE translation "I am usually/always not listening." Rochelle's use of the habitual be is another example of the AAL tense and aspect system. In addition to the habitual be, Rochelle also used the AAL expression "people call me out my name," a phrase meaning when people insult or slander you.[6]

Lexicon

In addition to demonstrating AAL grammatical structures, verbal interactions between African American youth at South Vista were also laden with the AAL lexicon. One afternoon I was shooting hoops with Sharon and Miles. Miles was wearing his white socks pulled up high, a retro look used by many NBA players.

> DJANGO: "You got the old school look."
> SHARON: "No, he *do* that because he ø *hella ashy.*"
> MILES: "No, it's like Baron Davis."
> Sharon shakes her head. "You ø *ashy,*" she says and she walks off.
> (April 2, 2007)

In addition to the AAL optional *absence of 3rd person singular "s"* (or, here, "es") in "do" for the DAE "does," Sharon also omitted the copula twice in "he ø hella ashy" and "You ø ashy." Yet grammar was not at the center of this interaction: the exchange hinged on the term "ashy." Although there is much debate about what constitutes the AAL lexicon, "ashy" is considered a long-standing AAL in-group term. It is a generally negative term for dry skin that is uncared for. Sharon was calling Miles out for not taking care of his legs with moisture lotion. She even increased the stakes by calling Miles "hella ashy," using the regional adjective "hella" for "extremely." Miles protested that he was looking like Baron Davis, a pro basketball player, but Sharon was not having it, ending the exchange by restating her claim and walking away.

Signifying and ritual insult

Beyond AAL grammar and lexicon, the African American youth I worked with at South Vista participated in broader speech traditions of Black language. One common speech act was *the dozens*, also known in the literature as *capping*.[7] An extended form of *signifying*, or using "verbal hyperbole, irony, indirection, metaphor, and the semantically unexpected" (Smitherman, 2006, p.70), the dozens are a form of ritual insult involving verbal word play centering on humorous insults to family members, friends, and the other participants. They are intended to be funny, often played to an audience. The following fieldnote I recorded in biology class shows Miles and his African American peer Derek engaged in playing ritual insults on each other. The class was studying DNA duplication when Miles asked a question.

MILES: "Why do people get mutations, deformities?"
TEACHER: "Sometimes they don't copy right."
MILES: "Then you end up short like Derek." The class laughs.
DEREK RETORTS: "Or dark like Miles." More laughter.
MILES: "Or like Sharon." More laughter. Sharon cuts her eyes at Miles, grinning. Miles shrinks back a bit, deciding he better not go further.

(February 28, 2007)

Miles asked his teacher a rather straightforward question, yet he asked the question seemingly to set up his planned cap on Derek's diminutive stature (as Derek was the shortest boy in tenth grade). Miles' comment was certainly unexpected, a sort of verbal juke that brought some laughter. Yet Derek knew how to play as well, and capped back remarking on Miles' dark skin (which was dark in the broader spectrum of African American skin pigment), only for Miles to pass it off on Sharon, who had a skin color similar to Miles. Sharon, although verbally silent, participated in the exchange by *cutting her eyes*, a recognized gesture of displeasure in the African Diaspora that can be as loud as words. While the crack about skin color may seem particularly mean-spirited and is certainly laden with the pain of racism, African American word play and humor has often served the function of flipping the painfully real White and internalized oppression into the humorous.[8] The fact that the relative darkness of skin has historically impacted and continues to impact the way African Americans view each other and are positioned by the dominant White culture is no laughing matter, yet to make it so at once masks the internalized shame and gives momentary relief from it. It is also important that I point out that all the people in the class, including the Latina teacher and myself, were people of color, which may make such a joke about skin color more possible.

The use of AAL grammar and lexicon, and participation in speech acts such as signifying sustained African American students' positions as members of the local and broader AAL speech community. Although social purposes and contexts varied in these examples, they were each acts of linguistic identity which placed youth within a tradition and a cultural community of "every Black person" being "bilingual." Rochelle and Miles, for example, often spoke of "our" or "my" language in our discussions about AAL. And yet, as I will show, both Miles and Rochelle understood that AAL was not theirs alone in the multiethnic youth space of South Vista. While these few moments from countless examples in my fieldwork show that AAL was alive and well among the African American youth of South Vista, my goal in this chapter is to illuminate something far less studied but nevertheless central to understanding the role of oral language in challenging and reinforcing ethnic difference and division in multiethnic schools and youth communities: how did Pacific Islanders and Latino/as also participate in AAL with Black youth and how did young people of all backgrounds make sense of this AAL sharing?

SHARING AAL AT SOUTH VISTA: GRAMMAR, LEXICON, AND RITUAL INSULT

Grammar

It was an afternoon walk I had taken often over my months at South Vista. On any given day I strolled over to the gym for practice with any number of the young people I was learning from. On this afternoon I was walking with Ela's cousin Soa and Cynthia, who was one of two Latinas on the team. There was an ease to our conversation that reflected many months of spending time together in the classroom and community. We talked about Derek, the team's point guard, who, despite his very small frame, was a favorite among many of the young women at South Vista.

CYNTHIA: "Derek's a *gangsta.*"
DJANGO: "A small *gangsta.*" We all chuckle.
CYNTHIA: "He *be teachin* everybody how to be *gangsta.*"
DJANGO: "What he *be teachin?*"
SOA: "He taught me how to smoke weed." They bust up
    laughing.
DJANGO: "Ok, that is something." I smile shaking my head.

(February 5, 2007)

Cynthia started the interaction with the Hip Hop lexical item *gangsta* (an action or state of being that rejects dominant rules, or an action or state of being that shows prowess or wealth).[9] I could not resist a small cap myself. Cynthia, a bilingual Latina, continued by employing the habitual be, that deep grammatical feature unique to AAL. I continued the participation, at which point Soa came with the unexpected and funny weed comment. While it is not my purpose here to debate the dangers or merits of Soa's comment (the teachers and administrators were aware of the prevalence of marijuana use), to be "gangsta" at South Vista meant resisting dominant rules of many kinds, both cultural preferences about how to speak and act, and those about what to do. While I struggled at times with some youth choices (e.g., truancy and substance use), I also worked to recognize them from youth perspectives. Linguistic resistance to DAE norms was certainly one major choice, a choice Cynthia made here by indexing youth identity through Hip Hop lexicon and AAL grammar. AAL grammar and lexicon, and the local Hip Hop lexicon, was also shared across ethnicity within the youth space of the classroom.[10] Back in biology class, Latina youth Sierra and Ela got into the mix. The class was testing light on earth worms by blasting flashlights on the squirming organisms. The worms, which do not relish bright light, thrashed about. "He ø goin dumb," observed Sierra. After some chuckles Ela agreed, "Hyphy," she said (January 10, 2007). In this interaction, Sierra omitted the copula and compared the worm's thrashing to a local dance known as "going dumb."[11] In a typical version of this dance, the dancers let their limbs go loose and shake, dipping up and down. Ela's agreement to Sierra's comment came through the more general term, "Hyphy," a regional movement of bass-heavy club tracks, dance moves, and local lexicon led by rappers such as E-40 and the deceased father of Hyphy, Mac Dre.

My ethnolinguistic interviews with Mexican/Mexican American and Pacific Islander youth also showed the use of many important AAL features (see Table 4).[12] Carlos, Rahul, and Ela all used the habitual be. Coupled with instances from my observations, this use of the tense/aspect system of AAL shows the ways many Latino/a and Pacific Islander youth had picked up an alternative sense of time and action in their everyday English – how they had come to embody June Jordan's (1985) wonderful statement about the relationship between (AAL) grammar and mind: "The syntax of a sentence equals the structure of your consciousness" (p. 163). In addition to the habitual be and other features I have previously discussed, Carlos, Carla, Rahul, and Julio used the existential it's in phrases like Carla's "It's some girls" for the DAE "There

Table 4. *AAL features from interviews of Latino/a and Pacific Islander youth*

Student	Feature	Examples
Carla	Zero copula	Next year my classes ø gonna be different
	Existential it is	*It's* some girls
Julio	Regularized agreement	People generally call you by the race *you is*
	Existential it is	*It's* really like nothing to do on my block
Carlos	Zero copula	You ø sorry
	Regularized agreement	Some dudes that *was* stealing cars
	Habitual be	Cause *they be trippin* about that
	Existential it is	*It was* a lot of Black people
Ela	Regularized agreement	That's how the teachers in Samoa *is*
	3rd person singular "s" / zero copula	Every time *he wake* up, he ø always turning
	Habitual be	My big *mouth be saying,* "Uh uh, uh uh"
	Multiple negation[13]	*I don't got no* "F" *I don't got no* "B"
Rahul	Existential it is	*It's* times you have to use it
	Regularized agreement	When you *was* growing up
	Zero copula	They ø keeping me on check
	Habitual be	We *be talking* about cars
	3rd person singular "s"	He just *come* in my room
	Multiple negation	I can't spit no rhyme

is/there are some girls."[14] They also employed the regularization of verb agreement patterns characteristic of AAL and other nondominant Englishes as in Carlos's, "Some dudes that *was* stealing cars."

Ela is a particularly interesting case of language sharing. Ela, who frequently used the habitual be, zero copula, multiple negation, regularization of verb agreement patterns, and absence of 3rd person singular "s," had arrived from American Samoa to South Vista only three years before our work together. Although these had been formative teenage years, to pick up and use grammatical features so often in her everyday English said a lot about the strong pull of AAL on Pacific Islander youth.

Lexicon

Beyond AAL grammar, participation by Pacific Islander and Latino/a youth in the AAL lexicon was pervasive in the multiethnic youth space of South Vista. Consider the following fieldnotes documenting uses of "ashy" in interethnic exchanges. The first example occurred in an exchange between Gloria, Miles, and me.

> I am sitting talking with Miles on the front benches. Gloria, who is wearing shorts, comes up to us and announces, "My legs are all *ashy*." Miles takes no notice of her comment, just glancing down at her legs.
>
> (March 20, 2007)

Another example of "ashy" was used in this extended exchange between Soa, Sharon, and Ricky.

> Soa and Sharon are sitting against a fence watching the boys play football. The girls are laughing and clowning the boys. I am standing with them and watching as well. Ricky runs out onto the field to play, tearing off his hoodie and throwing it down as he enters the field.

Soa: "Ricky, you better not take that off, your arms *is hella ashy!*" He is too far away to see if they are, in fact, ashy. Sharon shakes her head, "He ø *ashy.*" They laugh and I laugh with them. Soa launches into recounting what happened during geometry class. Ricky was near her and she looked over at his arms and "they *was hella ashy.*" She told him, "You better get some lotion." He went and asked African American student Rashida for lotion. Rashida told him he was *hella ashy* and gave it to him. We all laugh at the story.

(April 5, 2007)

The word "ashy" – used in the first example by a Mexican American to refer to herself and in the second example by a Samoan and an African American to refer to an African American – was used commonly in interethnic youth exchanges. These examples show participation in one of the most secure items in the AAL lexicon, a word that has long been seen as an exclusively in-group term between African Americans. While there is a long tradition of AAL-originated words (or meanings) making their way into mainstream popular use, the ratified sharing of "ashy" at South Vista showed a particularly deep linguistic connection between the youth of color at South Vista.

Signifying and ritual insult

In the above interaction, Soa used the lexical item "ashy" as a verbal game piece to cap on Ricky. By doing so Soa was not only employing the AAL lexicon, she was also participating in the ritual insult and verbal barbs characteristic of AAL speech acts such as signifying and the dozens. I witnessed many occasions when Latino/a and Pacific Islander youth entered these speech acts with their African American peers at South Vista. A prime example occurred early in the basketball season as I sat next to Julio and Miles as we stretched on the gym floor before practice.

Miles, "Mexican girls don't got no booty. It's all flat like." He smiles and shakes his head.

Julio feigns indignation, "Yes they do, they got booty!" He is also smiling.

Miles persists, "They don't got enough food in Mexico to have booties. They got to do the J-Lo and get it pumped in."

Julio retorts, "What about African girls, they don't got food neither."

Miles has the last word, "It's in the bone structure, though, they just got booty." And both bust up.

(November 8, 2006)

These "Mexican" versus "African" or "Black" dozens sessions were common between Latino and African American males who shared social networks. In this session on the gym floor the subject (or subjection) was women's bodies, although it was often wealth, employment status, and residency status. Here, Miles capped on what he deemed to be the unattractive bodies (specifically, rear ends) of an entire population of women. Julio protested. Miles, quick with the verbally unexpected, got two caps in. The first was that there wasn't enough food in Julio's homeland. The second was that the popular Latina superstar Jennifer Lopez, renowned in popular media for her attractive body (and specifically rear end), had to have surgery to be so good looking.[15] Julio came back with a cap about the lack of food in Africa, but Miles had an answer for that, too, ending the exchange by taking up the racist/sexist mythology of Black female body structure.[16]

It would be easy to continue in this vein, analyzing the racist/sexist content of this exchange, and objectification was paramount to the content of the ritual insult. I see no analytic "out" for Miles and Julio on this count, save the point that both seemed to feel a racialized-sexualized allegiance to women from their ethnic backgrounds. A possible additional saving grace; Miles' comment about "bone structure" can be seen as another example of flipping pain and racist stereotype into an (objectified) appreciation. He saw a sexualized beauty in the Black female body and seemed to be attempting here to argue for the superiority of such beauty, thus reinterpreting the racist stereotype for purposes of sexualized in-group solidarity. But there were other themes about national origin and poverty that provided an important subtext to the turning of pain and shame and racism into humor. Although I found myself struggling to listen to this particular exchange (though I did have to laugh at the genius of the J-Lo comment), it represents Julio's participation with Miles in AAL verbal word play that explicitly discussed difference.

One interpretation of such speech events could be that they were playing out community and national tensions between Latino/as and African Americans, dividing them as they struggled for the scarce resources of the oppressed in changing urban landscapes. I believe such an interpretation would be a dominant, divide-and-conquer reading, though. Given an understanding of the role of ritual insult in building and sustaining relationships between people, and between people and their language, I am convinced that such loaded insult sessions provided the opposite function: that is, they helped make humor out of shame and pain by unifying Latino/a and African American youth in shared practice and marginalization. In doing so, these sessions resisted both popular conceptions of African American/Latino/a relations and, by invoking stereotypical rhetorics of body, skin, wealth, and gender, they resisted a racist legacy by showing such rhetorics as ridiculous or flipping them into compliments.[17] Although much of this work of resistance was below the level of consciousness for Miles and Julio, both young men understood these sessions as humor about stereotypes within the genre of ritual insult. Each spoke about this in separate interviews when I asked them about these kinds of interactions.

> JULIO: I be like, "You wanna work in my cotton field?" And he be like, "When you gonna cut my grass?" It's just jokes; it's like

an inside joke or something like that. But, I mean, it's not to offend no one. It's just a way we get.

(January 26, 2007)

MILES: We have – not like arguments – but you know, friendly – They be like, "Black people this" and I be, "Mexican that," and then, you know, they'll go back, and it's funny. We're having fun.

(November 27, 2006)

I also observed Pacific Islander and Latina young women participating in AAL ritual insult with their African American peers at South Vista.[18] In this example (also laden with AAL grammar, morphology, and phonology), Ela signified on Miles as they worked in biology class to create Punnett squares (a diagram used to determine the probability of the genetic makeup for offspring). Miles was struggling to create his diagram using a ruler. Ela sat at the table behind him, and I was sitting behind Ela.

MILES: "It's crooked." He shakes his head looking down at his Punnett square.
ELA: "It would be." She chuckles and keeps working on her diagram.
MILES: "*I'ma* get you! Watch your back, Ela."
ELA: "*I'ma* a get Django on you."
MILES: "He *ain't* gonna do *nothin'*, he ø scared." He peers back at me with a smile.
DJANGO: "Please." Shaking my head, staring in mock intensity at Miles.
ELA: "Looks like you ø scared," She laughs at Miles who nods in defeat.[19]

(February 7, 2007)

Ela seized a moment of weakness by Miles to insult far more than his diagram. Her cap carried the broader meaning that Miles himself was crooked and unfit. Miles, within the play of the game, felt this and took a rather direct intimidation approach. Ela assessed all the verbal and physical tools available in her environment and chose to use me as a counterattack. Miles tried to call her bluff, but I was willing to play, too. My assist was just what Ela needed to finish Miles off. Not only was he "crooked," he was also now "scared."

While it is a significant research contribution to simply document the use of AAL grammar, lexicon, and speech acts in the everyday English of Latino/a and Pacific Islander youth, such participation alone did not tell me much about the ways AAL worked within the ethnic geography of difference, division, and unity at South Vista. Nor was it evident whether such uses were instances of general unratified crossing into AAL, or whether they were ratified by the African American in-group as shared practices. In my interviews with youth across groups I came to understand the processes involved in AAL use – that it was, by and large, seen by all parties as a shared linguistic repertoire across youth space. I also came to see how youth explained what AAL was and why so many youth used it as something of a lingua franca in multiethnic youth space.

"EVERYBODY SPEAKS THAT WAY": YOUTH UNDERSTANDINGS OF AAL SHARING

African American youth were keenly aware that their language was used by Latino/as and Pacific Islanders. Though this participation was generally seen as unproblematic and caused far more social cohesion than social fissures in youth space, during a mid-year interview Rochelle expressed reservations about some Latino/a AAL use.

> DJANGO: Does it bother you when you hear the Mexican kids talking kinda Black like that?
> ROCHELLE: Yeah.
> D: It does? Like when all of them do it, or just some of them? Like some of them it's okay, some of them it's not?

R: Some is okay because some be half-Black, and some dudes be trying to talk like that just to get the attention. It's not funny. They gonna get beat up.

(February 9, 2007)

Rochelle was aware that some Latino/a youth participated in AAL. Her explanation of when such use was ratified by African American youth was complex. Rochelle sanctioned some AAL use by "half-Black" Latino/as. She did not mean racially mixed youth (Rochelle did not have any Latino/a-Black biracial youth in her social network), but, rather, those Latino/as who she deemed were "real" AAL speakers versus those who were feigning prowess for attention. Those who were faking, warned Rochelle, might be physically threatened. Although Rochelle's comment was atypical and I never heard of or saw such violence take place at South Vista (or even an argument or comment over inauthentic AAL use), these possible inauthentic uses show that some AAL participation by Latino/a and Pacific Islander youth might be perceived as unratified language crossing rather than the more generally approved language sharing.

During an interview, Miles expressed a more general sentiment felt across ethnic groups at South Vista about AAL sharing. When I asked him what he thought about AAL use by Pacific Islander and Latino/a youth at South Vista, Miles spoke of a community socializing process in multiethnic youth space.

MILES: I'm not trippin. They're my homeboys, most of them. I'm cool with it. I don't think they're trying to steal anything. They're just being themselves because they were born here and raised here, but they were also born and raised in their house, so they can – they get the best of both worlds, I guess.

(November 27, 2006)

Miles saw AAL use as a shared part of South Vista youth space. In fact, for Miles, such sharing promoted friendship across ethnicity, promoted Latino/a AAL speakers to be his "homeboys." Miles did not feel these ratified speakers were taking his language. Instead, he saw them as "being themselves," youth who grew up in an AAL-speaking environment with African American peers. Though by saying "Most of them" Miles left the possibility open that some use could be inauthentic, the general thrust of his understanding was that AAL sharing was part of a community socializing process involving sustained linguistic and cultural contact between South Vista's ethnic communities. Even though Miles understood this, he also displayed some envy about the Spanish-speaking abilities of his peers. They got to speak his language, the shared language of multiethnic youth space, and also got to know the omnipresent Spanish, spoken by 70 percent of his school and community. They got "the best of both worlds," a view that displays the envy and desire for Spanish proficiency by African American and Pacific Islander youth that I explored in Chapter 2.

This was not the only time Miles described this view of the community socializing process of AAL sharing. In a later interview, he furthered this notion.

MILES: There's a lot of us in there that talk [AAL], well, not a lot, but you know, it's like for you who dress like they're Black, you know, with the Girbauds, the long T's, you know. And there's some and they just speak *slang* like regular Black people. It's like they were grown up here and it makes it cool at the same time.

(March 26, 2007)

This statement fell in line with the socializing view of sharing. As he said, "They were grown up here." Yet Miles provided two further understandings here. One is the way he tied AAL use to other cultural ways of being, other identity markers of Blackness in youth space. Here, Miles used clothing as a prime marker. Girbaud, the hottest urban jean designer of the year, and long T-shirts were ways of indexing participation in Black cultural discourse. This way of dressing coupled with "slang" made Latino/a and Pacific Islander AAL speakers "like regular Black people."

Latino/a and Pacific Islander youth I interviewed also attached AAL sharing to particular cultural activities. Julio, for instance, described his participation on the predominantly African American basketball team as a forum for speaking AAL. Rahul, who wrote and performed raps, talked of his role as an emcee as sharing in linguistic practices across race. These uses, attached to particular cultural activities, were generally ratified as appropriate by the African American in-group. It seemed such ratification hinged on the speaker showing prowess in the given activity. Rahul's ability to rap, for example, was deemed considerable by the Black peers he rhymed with, as was Julio's relative skill on the basketball court by the African American players on his team.

One statement Miles made summed up his view of linguistic socialization and sharing; "Since they're in my culture, they speak the same way" (November 27, 2006). Miles and Rochelle felt ownership and solidarity about their culture and language. Yet they also realized they shared that culture with the large and increasing number of Latino/as and with Pacific Islanders who "were grown up here." This was an awareness about AAL that Pacific Islander and Latino/a youth also had at South Vista. Ela, for instance, was clear that she and her Samoan peers used AAL as their everyday English, as she told me during our January interview.

> DJANGO: When you're not talking Samoan – when you're talking with your friends in English – how would you describe the way you guys talk?
>
> ELA: We talk *ghetto* a lot. Ghetto – like kids talk. They're like, "Man, he *be* cursing me – he's talking ghetto."
>
> (January 16, 2007)

Ela used the habitual be to give life to her description of what she called "ghetto." Other than "slang," "ghetto" was the most common term used by youth across groups to describe AAL. "Ghetto" at South Vista and in the broader urban youth and Hip Hop culture was an adjective to describe something as urban and generally dilapidated, though not always in a negative way. Depending on context, "ghetto" could be positive, negative, or relatively neutral. Ela's use here was rather neutral to describe a way of talk that was everyday between peers. Carlos also viewed AAL as the most common English used across youth space. When I asked him directly about whether African Americans had a different way with words, he shared this view.

> DJANGO: Would you say that African American people in general have a way of talking? You said they only talk English. Do they talk English like everybody else or is their English different in any way?
>
> CARLOS: No, well they actually talk like everybody from South Vista, they talk *slang*, at least a little that you could tell, but they speak like that, too. So everybody here speaks the same in terms of the English.
>
> (January 22, 2007)

As Carlos considered my question he came to the conclusion that "everybody here speaks the same in terms of English," everybody speaks "slang." During a later March interview I had with Carlos he provided maybe the most succinct statement of AAL linguistic socialization at South Vista. Carlos, who had come to South Vista from Michoacán, Mexico in 1999, spoke very little English when he arrived in the United States. As he shared his personal story of learning English mainly from Black youth in his first South Vista middle school, he came to this general statement.

> CARLOS: What happens is, like, when kids are coming – like English learners, since they're around Black people sometimes, they learn the slang instead of, like, the English-English.
>
> (March 12, 2007)

Like Miles, Carlos realized that youth learning English in South Vista were likely to learn English within the long-standing African American community of South Vista. While Miles spoke of those

Latino/a and Pacific Islander youth who were born in South Vista, Carlos added the perspective of immigrants, like himself and Ela, who learned to share in Black speech as they learned to navigate a new city, a new country, a new language, and a new, hybrid identity.

I was surprised by the scope and depth of AAL use by Pacific Islander and Latino/a youth in the multiethnic space of South Vista. I worked to capture the ways these youth displayed linguistic dexterity through various levels of AAL, in grammar, lexicon, and ritual insult. Beyond capturing practice, I was interested in the linguistic plurality – the ways youth made sense of the sharing and crossing that went on – and how AAL use across groups challenged and reinforced ethnic division. And there were many surprises here, too, which offer great potential for classroom practice and for visions of pluralism in multiethnic communities. Yet nothing surprised me as deeply as the pervasive use of the N-words[20] within and across groups at South Vista. It was not the use of the words, or the semantic flexibility of the words, that stunned me. Rather, it was the degree of use by Latino/a and Pacific Islander youth that I was little prepared for. Early in the year I made a decision to attempt to understand the N-words in this multiethnic context. I felt I owed it to myself, to the research community, and to the youth who spoke, often unprompted, about the semantics and politics of the N-words, to uncover the workings of the painful and often misunderstood words as they lived in the minds and voices of South Vista's young people.

"THIS IS THE NEW MEANING": THE N-WORDS IN MULTIETHNIC CONTEXT

It was early September 2006, my first of dozens of visits to Carlos and Julio's eleventh grade English class. Students were milling around, slowly settling into their desks. I had barely situated myself at the back table when Latino student C.C. made his entrance onto the scene. C.C., wearing a long T-shirt with "California Hyphy" emblazoned across the front, strode around the room looking for a choice desk. "I need to sit with a good *nigga!*" he announced. I looked around the room and saw only two African American students, Jamal and Dexter, and it didn't appear that C.C. was addressing them specifically. C.C. repeated his call twice more, "I need me a good *nigga* to sit with." He looked at his friend Manuel, "No, not you." He carried on another moment before finding a seat and neighbor he felt was good enough.

It was clear to me even in the first overt use of this particular N-word I heard at South Vista that C.C. did not mean the derogatory definitions many attribute universally to the word. It was also clear that he was not addressing only African Americans, but rather the broader community of (male?) youth in the classroom. What was not yet clear to me was how Jamal and Dexter may have felt about this use and, more generally, what the pragmatics and semantics of the N-words were in this multiethnic youth space. How did this most controversial of English words – laden as it is with the legacy of US slavery, racism, and White oppression against African Americans – play a role in challenging and reinforcing ethnic difference and division at South Vista? As I typed up my fieldnotes that September evening I struggled to come to terms with C.C.'s nonchalant, seemingly neutral use of the N-word. I decided to attend to uses of the N-words in my research and, as well, to see if I could get at youth understandings of its meaning in this multiethnic community of color.

Over my year with the youth of South Vista I heard and recorded hundreds of uses of the various incarnations of the N-words. I heard them between every combination of ethnicity and gender possible at the school and in the community. I will provide some extended interview excerpts in this section as youth sense-making about the N-words was extraordinarily complex. I will set this youth theorizing alongside examples from youth space to give social life to their understandings. I begin with Miles' rich comments from our November interview when I asked him about the local lexical item "rogue," a term generally used between males as a term of endearment.

DJANGO: So what does "rogue," mean to you?

MILES: "Rogue" is just like "dude." You know how White people say, "Dude this?" Something like that. But I know what the real definition means, like "a criminal" or something like that. You know, but we use it as a different term. You know, we change the meaning. It's kind of like the word "nigga." You know, we say "nigga" but we actually put a positive twist on it, meaning "dude," instead of having it be this negative word that nobody says. You know, we changed it and said, "This is the new meaning of it."

D: What do you mean, changed the meaning of it? What was the other meaning of it?

M: It's a derogatory term for Black people. You know, the ignorant person. Back in the '60s, you know. They used that word for a derogatory slang usage.

D: Right. And so you changed it? And so when you use it with your friends, what does it mean, exactly?

M: It mean like, "dude," "rogue," – and not just me but you know, I think, as a whole. And the whole Black community has changed it all over America, not just this area. It means, just like, "Nigga, come here", not like, "Nigger!" Not like that.

D: So would you use it with people that weren't Black?

M: Hispanic people. I use it with Hispanic people, you know. And they use it too – that's why I don't trip over them using it. Now I've got in a couple of fights because of a White person who said it. I'm not going to lie – I told them, "Don't say that." I used to go to a White school and I've heard it from them a couple times. And I've got in fights and been suspended over it. And they didn't get suspended. And so things like that, I don't understand. I understand that it's just for us, you know. You don't use it. You've used that word, you've used it out. You can't say it no more.

D: "You've used it out." What do you mean by that? I think I know, but …

M: You used it out. After you put your meaning, I think – if I
hear a White person say, *"Nigger,"* it automatically brings back
memories as in what you put my people through back in the
day. But when I hear a Black person say it, it doesn't bring back
memories, it's just like a common term between us.

(November 27, 2006)

I did not have to ask Miles directly about the N-words to elicit his
extended, complex understanding. Miles launched into an explanation of the centuries-old African American practice of changing
negative words and putting "a positive twist" on them rather than
having negative words "that nobody uses."[21] Miles was quite aware
that the word can and still does have derogatory meanings. He hark-
ened back to the "1960s" and "back in the day" as a time when this
oppressive, racist meaning used by White people against Black people
was the only meaning. Miles understood the change in meaning as
a collective action of the Black community across America. He jux-
taposed *"Nigga,* come here" with *"Nigger!"* making an exaggerated
phonological difference in realizing the final "r." Miles made a clear
semantic distinction between at least two words here. Although I
will show more meanings than these two in youth space, "nigga"
and "nigger" was the major separation between the "common term"
and the derogatory one.[22]

Miles did not see the common N-word as a term exclusively
for African American use. He would not have tripped at C.C.'s use
and saw such Latino/a uses as acceptable and usual. However, it was
only youth of color who could share the term. He recounted conflicts
with White students who used the N-words in the middle school he
had been bused to from South Vista. These conflicts had resulted in
further injustice from Miles' point of view, an injustice that further
added to White students being barred from using N-words. White
people could not participate anymore. Miles pronounced their use
"nigger," which brought back memories of slavery, a flood of painful history which Miles was unwilling to let happen. While African

Americans had changed the meaning between themselves and, in multiethnic youth space, between youth of color, White folks had "used it out."

Here is one example from scores in my fieldnotes and recordings showing the common use of "nigga" as "friend" in an interethnic exchange. I was standing by some redwood trees near the school parking lot with African American student Terrence one day after school. Rahul came up and commented on Terrence's shirt, a throwback Kobe Bryant Lakers jersey.

> RAHUL: "That shirt *go*, it *hella go*. Where did you get it?"
> TERRENCE: "You got one, too, *nigga*."
> RAHUL: "Nah, I got the purple and yellow one. It's *hoot*."
>
> (April 5, 2007)

In addition to uses of the local lexical items "go" (to look, sound, or be excellent) and "hoot" (to be lame or unfavorable), Terrence casually used an N-word here across ethnic difference with his Fijian Indian peer to mean "friend."

Beyond the race of the speaker and the pronunciation of the words, Miles commented later in the same interview on generation and gender as additional constraints to the use of the N-words. In the following excerpt, I asked him about his White basketball coach's rule about not using the words. The coach, a very dedicated man who took players home after practice and spent weekends with them in the gym, had proclaimed several times with a rather convoluted rationale that the word was not to be used on the court. As a reason, he said referees would call a technical foul and "until it's equal and everyone can use it, nobody can." Miles was unconcerned with the details of the rule.

> MILES: He does not like the word, so I respect that. Because if he doesn't like the word that kind of shows something on his behalf, that no racism's between them, you know.
> DJANGO: Do you think it would be different if it was a Black coach?

M: Actually, I've had a couple Black coaches say, "Don't say that word." But then I've had a couple of Black coaches that say it's all right. You know, everybody uses it theirselves, so it depends. It just depends on their mindset. It's kind of how old they are, also.

D: What do you mean by that?

M: If my coach is 60 and he's Black; he went through that *"nigger"* phase. You know, people called him that. Then he would be like, "No, you're not using that." But if I had a 30-year-old coach who was saying it – and he's listening to rap – *"Nigga, yeah"* – it would be a different story. So I think it just depends on who the person is, their mindset, and the way they think. You know, what they been through.

D: And do you only use it with guys?

M: Pretty much. You know, I don't really use it with girls. But then girls use it with everybody. Girls, dude, it doesn't matter. But pretty much I just use it with homeboys, my real friends.

(November 27, 2006)

Miles did some further layering of the general workings of the N-words here. The first was that his coach's rule actually showed respect because Miles knew that his coach, a 60-year-old White man, understood the word only in its derogatory manner. This fit well with his proclamation that White people had used it up. Why would this White person be any different? His coach could only use the derogatory meaning and, for Miles, could only understand it in this derogatory meaning.

Beyond race, Miles also knew that pragmatics and semantics were generational. An older Black man who had gone "through that 'nigger' phase" was not part of the change that had happened since then. For this older Black man, the N-words could not be used by African American or White speakers. A younger Black man, say 30, had been part of the shift in meanings and use forwarded most aggressively through Hip Hop culture. He would be fine with common between-Black uses of the N-words.

A final comment from Miles was about gender and use. Male and female youth of all ethnicities generally agreed with Miles' point that males did not use the N-words with female youth regularly. Rahul, for example, saw the gender division as well. During an early interview he explained that as a non-Black youth the stakes were high for him in this regard. He recounted times when African American girls protested uses of the N-words in middle school. As a result, he was careful not to use them with African American young women.

> RAHUL: So I never actually said it in front them [Black girls]. You know, once in a while [I use it with] my Mexican friends, some of my Black friends, you know. Mostly boys, they don't really mind at all. It's the girls that come up tripping.
>
> DJANGO: So even Black boys don't mind?
>
> R: They don't mind. I say, you know, "What's going on, *nigga*?"
>
> (October 27, 2006)

Rahul, who here was speaking of the N-word as a term of endearment, would not use it in any form toward African American young women. In fact, I heard very few examples of males, African American or not, calling females the N-words. It is also true that male use in general dominated in my observations of youth space, though I do have examples of African American, Latina, and Pacific Islander young women using the N-words with young men across ethnicity. Here are two quick instances from my fieldnotes. I overheard the first exchange between Latino student Rudolfo and Tongan student Meto in the hall in between classes. The second was a rhythmic, flirtatious back and forth exchange between Latina student Sierra and African American student Gerald at the beginning of first-period biology class.

> METO: "I seen your girl."
>
> RUDOLFO: "She ain't my girl."
>
> METO: "She's yo girl, *nigga*."
>
> (April 17, 2007)

SIERRA: "Gerald came to school! *Nigga,* whaaat?" She moves
toward him.

GERALD: "Whaaat?" And he moves toward her.

SIERRA: *"Nigga,* whaaat?" She moves toward him more.

GERALD: "Whaaat?" And they both smile broadly.

(December 8, 2006)

The distinctions between derogatory and non-derogatory pronunciations were not merely understood by South Vista youth, the African
American youth in my observations also practiced these distinctions. Although the vast majority of uses at South Vista were Miles'
"common term" variety, the derogatory pronunciation with the "r"
fully realized was used occasionally by Black youth either to mock
other African American youth while simultaneously ridiculing
racist stereotypes or to recount injustice. As I sat out on the bench
with Ela during a mid-year interview, Anthony suddenly entered the
picture. He had been sent out of class by a White teacher and shouted
out the injustice to us from some twenty yards away.

ANTHONY: "Yo Django! Ms T. don't like *niggers!"* He walks
toward us.

ELA: *"Niggers?"*

ANTHONY (who is next to us now): "She don't like *niggers,* or
niggas, or *niggahs!"* He exaggerates the last pronunciation for
effect.

ELA: "Or *negroes!"* Ela is with him now.

ANTHONY: "Or *negroes* especially. I'm a *negro!"* He nods his
head.

(March 5, 2007)

I witnessed other occasions when Black male youth used "nigger" to
describe the perceptions or disciplinary tactics of teachers (none of
whom were African American). Here, Anthony used the full range of
pronunciations (going a bit overboard with the exaggerated "niggah")
to show that his teacher didn't like African Americans no matter

which N-word was used. Ela showed some solidarity here, extending the list with "negroes," the antiquated term that has come back into use somewhat as a marker of Black pride. Anthony took some solace in Ela's solidarity; "I'm a negro," he said, and seemed to regain a sense of pride.

The "r" variety N-word was also used in mocking between African American youth at South Vista. Such uses were rare in my observations and always came with a *marked* White phonology characteristic of the Black comedic tradition.[23] I witnessed one example of this mock derogatory N-word between African American youth Sharon and Derek during a mixed gender (and mixed ethnicity) basketball game on February 2nd, 2007. "Make the shot, *nigger*," Sharon said to Derek. "Pass me the ball, *nigger*," Derek said to Sharon. Both youth smiled broadly as they tossed around the mock racial slur in hyperbolic White voice. This use, complex in its pairing with marked White speech, played into the larger tradition of using ritual insult and White mimicry to flip pain, shame, and a racist world into a complex humor. It was a humor that embodied the legacy of the White supremacist origins of the N-word and of the slave–master relationship, possibly resisting that legacy by showing it as ridiculous and laughable.[24]

I should reinforce the point that, in my observations, Latino/a and Pacific Islander youth did not use the derogatory pronunciation of the N-word in multiethnic youth space to mock, to report injustice, or for any other reason. However, it would be a mistake to assume that youth across groups always meant "friend," or even the more neutral "person" when using the N-words with their peers. During one interview with Ela, we were talking about her often combative, flirtatious relationship with Ricky and the ritual insults they hurled at each other regularly.

> ELA: He be talking shit to me for no reason. He be like, "Hey,
> *nigga*. Fuck you!" I be like, "What the hell – go out and
> fuck your own-self!" [Then he says] "Okay, I'm scared of
> you – okay."

D: So he uses the word "nigga" with you?

E: Sometimes. Yeah, he been saying that, too, but I don't trip.

D: No, no, no. What do you think that word means when he says it?

E: Black slave.

D: You think that's what he's saying?

E: Uh-huh.

D: You think that's always what people mean when they say that word?

E: No ... I think he was just playing around. He's been saying that a lot, but we don't trip.

D: No, no, no. I'm not saying you trip and I'm not tripping either, but do you think he always means "slave" when he says it?

E: No.

D: Okay, what else might he mean? Like when he says, "What's going on, nigga?"

E: That you're dumb – something like that.

D: Okay, do you ever use it?

E: Sometimes.

D: And so what do you mean when you say it – like honestly?

E: When I say it, it's like "dumb" – like, "Nigga, shut up!" – stuff like that.

(January 16, 2007)

In Ela's description of her interactions with Ricky, she recalled him using the N-word with her. When I asked what she thought he meant, her first response was "Black slave," certainly a possibility, though it would most likely have been the derogatory pronunciation if that was Ricky's meaning. A more likely meaning was the negative, but not derogatory use of "nigga" between youth of color in the youth space of South Vista. "Nigga," it turned out, had several possible meanings depending on communicative context, from "friend," to "person," to "jerk." It is also important to remember that Ela had only arrived in the United States from Samoa a few years before our work together. Though she shared heavily in AAL, Ela was probably still learning the historic, racist, and contemporary nuances of the N-words. When pushed, Ela came up with the meaning she often used in my observations, "dumb" person or "jerk." Let me provide a quick example from basketball practice on April 6th, 2007. Ela had just come out from changing into her basketball clothes when Latino youth Juan cracked, "Yo legs is hella ashy" and started chuckling.[25] Ela wasn't having it, "Fuck you, *nigga!*" she retorted.

Carla provided the most disturbing take on the N-words during our December interview. She began by telling me that her older brothers used the term with each other. This use by Latino youth was hardly surprising to me given my observations. Yet, as her description went on, Carla showed that the most derogatory of meanings of the N-words were still alive at South Vista, even if they weren't used in the multiethnic youth space of school.

> CARLA: Yeah, they call each other that, and they even call my mom, only when my mom is in a good mood. Yeah, my second older brother, he would be like, "*Nigger*, go get me some food!" or, "*Nigger*, today!" But I even a lot of times use it on my mom, you know, "*Nigger*, whatever!"
>
> DJANGO: And so when you say it what do you mean by the word?
>
> C: Black person.
>
> D: So you're saying basically to your mom, "Black person, do the dishes," or whatever?
>
> C: Yeah.
>
> D: So why are you saying that?
>
> C: Just to play around. Yeah, but I just say it when we're in the house. Because if I say it when I'm on the street or something like that, they would get mad at me.
>
> D: They would get mad at you.
>
> C: Yeah, and I don't want problems.
>
> (December 12, 2006)

Carla's comments are important on many levels. First, she used the derogatory pronunciation and meaning with her brothers and mom in cruel jokes about housework and subservience, in deep ways reenacting the legacy of slavery and reinforcing painful racial divisions. Yet Carla, who was born in Mexico and had lived the majority of her life in South Vista, admitted she would never use the N-word this way (or possibly any way – I have no record of her using it at school) outside her home. She knew that African Americans would be upset at this use and it would cause friction. I do not want to imply that this derogatory use was common, for Carla or anyone else, and her brothers probably used the N-words in less offensive ways, too. As I already stated, I never witnessed or heard about this pronunciation or meaning by Pacific Islanders and Latino/as in youth space or in my observations in the community. Yet the presence of this use, even isolated, has important implications I will take up in the conclusion to this section.

I did not use the N-words myself in my everyday interactions with youth inside or outside classrooms. Although the N-words were, to a relatively minor extent, part of my social world during my teenage and college years through my participation in basketball and Hip Hop culture, I did not grow up using the words regularly and to do so at South Vista would have been inauthentic and inappropriate. As the year wore on, however, male youth of all ethnicities did occasionally use the N-word as a term of endearment with me, a light-skinned Black/White biracial man in my mid 30s. Terrence, for instance, came up to me with a huge smile one April day and said, "Yo *nigga*, I met this girl, man. She is so fine, *nigga!*" This use in some ways increases the validity of youth comments with me and of the participant observations I made with them over time. I mention it for another reason, though; I appreciated the term used in this way toward me and it showed me deeply what it could mean to youth across race and ethnicity at South Vista. And, set against all its horrific history and continuing hatefulness, what it did mean to so many of them.

AAL was shared across ethnicity by many youth at South Vista. Part of this sharing was sharing the lexicon, both local and national, both painful and playful. The N-words, possibly the most loaded of all words in the English language, were part of this shared language. It had many meanings and two distinct pronunciations. The vast majority of uses meant "friend" or "brother." As Miles said, "This is the new meaning of it." Smitherman (2006) provides an eloquent summation of what is sure to become a classic essay on the N-words:

> Nigga is from the lexicon of the counterlanguage that African Americans have created over the centuries, turning the White man's language upon its head, transforming *bad* into *good*. The impact of words depends on who is saying what to whom, under what conditions, and with what intentions. Meanings reside in the speakers of language.
>
> (p. 51, italics in original)

And yet even though Smitherman's wise words rang true in the youth space of South Vista, her essay is missing one key feature: multiethnicity. Of the vast research and writing on the N-words,[26] none has looked into the way it is used by youth of color across ethnicity. In fact, only two chapters I know of even mention in passing that it is used across youth ethnic groups.[27] There is good reason for this. The word was born out of White supremacy and the enslavement of African Americans. Yet contexts like South Vista offer another window into the storied and painful term that must be understood. The N-words, like AAL more broadly, are not Black and White anymore.

Understanding how the N-words are used in multiethnic contexts like South Vista can show us the complex semantics and pragmatics youth navigate and can also show us where crucial tensions and misunderstandings remain. Miles, who understood much about the various meanings and ratified the N-words used by his Latino friends, did not mention that the stakes for using the N-words are different for Black youth than for other youth of color. After all, the word originated as a term of racist supremacy about African Americans and is intimately tied with that history. Although other youth of color could use it in Miles' scheme, it would be a mistake to think their historical and continuing relationship with the N-words was the same. It is true, of course, that all the communities of color in South Vista have historically struggled and continue the struggle against racist policies and ideologies in the United States. My point here, though, is that while sharing in uses of the N-words does show a close linguistic connection and common marginalization, it must also be seen in the larger context of linguistic and racial history. Ela, a relatively new immigrant to the United States and South Vista, was somewhat unsure about the various meanings and how they related to slavery. Rahul was careful not to use the N-words in the presence of African American young women. And, of course, Carla re-enacted painful oppression with little of the critical edge seen in some of the other humor I have analyzed in this chapter.

Most simply, researchers and educators need to understand the N-words because they remain a source of major contention between youth, between youth and their teachers, and between youth and their communities. I witnessed and heard about many conflicts over the N-words between youth and adults at the school: a White bus driver kicking a Black student off for using the N-words; a Latina teacher threatening to call home if she heard the N-words; a White coach barring the N-words from the court; a White teacher calling penalties for uses of the N-words during a staff–student flag foot-ball game. Never in my observations did the dedicated teachers and adults at the school take the word on in the complexity it embodied in multiethnic youth space.

I am not arguing for unhistoricized and uncritical uses of the N-words, or even that adults should allow young people to use the words inside or outside classrooms. What my time in South Vista showed me, however, was that youth across ethnicity had rich understandings and nuanced ways of using the N-words. They also sometimes participated in painful uses and were unsure of the rules and of who they might offend. What I am arguing is that our answers inside and outside school need to meet youth theorizing and prob-lematizing with the sort of historical and contemporary study they deserve. This means taking the N-words on directly in historical and pop cultural study inside classrooms. It means allowing contemporary thinking from sociolinguistics and Hip Hop culture to be studied alongside the horrific origins, histories, and continuing derogatory uses of the N-words. Carla needed this. And so did Sharon and Derek and all the youth who navigated the many meanings of the N-words. And, for that matter, so did the coach and the teachers. In fact, maybe they needed it most of all.

AAL AND EDUCATION IN MULTIETHNIC SCHOOLS

AAL was a primary way with words used by African American youth at South Vista. And it was battling for the hearts and voices of many Pacific Islander and Latino/a youth as well. AAL was a major player in the work of forging dexterous identities for youth like Ela, Carlos, and Rahul, and it offers important lessons for multiethnic schools and understandings of pluralist cultural spaces.

Although youth were generally aware that AAL was a Black-originated language style, it had become a shared practice that worked more to challenge notions of ethnic difference and division than to reinforce them. While Spanish and, less so, Pacific Islander languages often worked to forge in-group solidarity and reinforce ethnic difference and division in positive and difficult ways, AAL use tended to unite youth across groups. AAL use showed a pluralist tendency toward shared practices, the other necessary half of the paradox of pluralism. AAL provided a sense of being from South Vista, and using the terms (like "ashy or "nigga"), the constructions (like the habitual be or zero copula), and the speech events (like ritual insult) of AAL provided a shared space of prestige against the backdrop of shared marginalization in a society dominated by a White language and culture. It was a shared counterlanguage that resisted dominant norms even as it failed to eclipse their ultimate power.

You will remember Miles' statement I discussed in the prologue to the chapters, "We all gotta stay together. We're the minorities."

AAL was the primary linguistic practice of cultural togetherness. Yet, even as AAL was a tool of interethnic solidarity, it was somewhat troubling that Black youth were the only group that did not have a space of ethnic and linguistic safe haven in multiethnic youth space. Sure, African American youth could exclude non-AAL speakers from the meanings of certain words, constructions, and speech events and did so (often at their peril) to teachers. Yet while most Latino/a and Pacific Islander youth could retreat into an important space of in-group solidarity through practicing their own linguistic and cultural heritage, when African American youth used AAL it was likely that youth of other ethnic groups got their meanings and would join in. And African American originated clothing and music were also shared across groups.

I struggled with this tension: AAL as unifier on one end, Black youth with few safe havens of in-group solidarity to communicate exclusively together in youth space on the other. This tension certainly goes beyond language. Current demographic shifts in South Vista and in urban communities nationally forecast an ever shrinking urban presence for the African American population.[28] With these shrinking numbers at South Vista came shrinking exclusively owned practices. This tension was playing out in the lives of Rochelle and Miles and their Pacific Islander and Latino/a peers. They theorized about what it meant and, ultimately, saw the speaking on the wall: AAL would be shared just as their community was shared. A generation before, South Vista had been a predominantly Black community. In the face of demographic changes, AAL was echoing across social space from previous eras and South Vista's African American youth were, in a sense, carriers of the linguistic and cultural torch from the Black city their parents had grown up in only decades before. These young people were passing their language into youth space and, through sharing it, ensuring its interethnic survival and importance in the community.

The tension between AAL as unifier and the lack of African American youth safe haven for in-group solidarity would not be so bothersome if all youth knew more about the structure and history of AAL. While African American youth did take a certain amount of pride in others being part of their music and their culture, they also struggled with the false linguistic shame of seeing their shared language practices as simply "slang" and "ghetto."[29] School is in an ideal position to be the site of critical language learning that could bolster the pride of African American youth about their linguistic heritage while simultaneously fostering more conscious respect from youth of other backgrounds, many of whom participate in AAL. To be clear, I do not mean to imply that youth were not aware of the local and (through Hip Hop) global prestige of AAL, but rather that more consciousness would have raised the level of respect for the language and its speakers. This is a respect the African American youth in my work could certainly have used to bolster their position as important members of the youth community and of their city.

None of this erodes the fact that AAL *was* a unifier in youth space. It worked to help youth, both consciously and unconsciously, move across divisions predicated on ethnic difference and seek common ground in an oppressive world. Unfortunately, school did not treat AAL as a unifier. In fact, school did not seem to treat AAL much at all. Although I witnessed one attempt to use rap as a cultural entry point in an English class, the caring and well-qualified teachers of South Vista did not work with AAL grammar or lexicon during my year of observations. While I also did not witness the old school corrections of AAL speech that haunted previous eras (no teachers shouting, "It's not 'she in school!' it's 'she *is* in school!'") and South Vista teachers generally valued and attended to difference, there was no mention that a grammar was happening inside and outside the classroom across ethnicity. Just as exclusion, solidarity, crossing, and sharing in Spanish and Pacific Islander languages went virtually unaddressed, so too did the sharing of AAL. This was saddening to me. We dedicate entire classes to learning English, but teachers, their curriculum, and broader structures of teacher preparation are ill equipped to use the Englishes of our students as critical resources in learning. Teacher education must contend with the demographic and linguistic realities of changing urban communities, and AAL will remain a central player in these changes.

Our research into using AAL as just such a resource for learning is vast. We know how to use AAL structures to contrast them with DAE structures so that students come to see and attend to the differences depending on social context and purpose. We know much about the ways the features I have shown in the youth space of South Vista carry into student writing. We also know what it looks like to teach African American AAL-speaking students to maintain cultural competence while acquiring DAE.[30]

Yet our research has remained amazingly Black and White. My work with the youth of South Vista suggests that we must reconsider where our vast linguistic and educational knowledge of AAL should be used. Although the teachers of South Vista taught in a predominantly Latino/a school, the student demographics belied the linguistic reality. Teachers needed knowledge of AAL just as they needed knowledge of other heritage languages, like Spanish and Samoan. This knowledge would have revealed an amazing tapestry of practices which reached across groups to claim a linguistic and cultural plurality that often resisted traditional visions of racial strife in schools and communities. Such plurality sometimes seeped into classroom space, but usually operated below the official script of classroom learning. Yet it begged to be given official academic space to foster and to extend youth understandings of plural schools and plural communities.

Such a classroom space would embody the pedagogy of pluralism I have mentioned throughout this book – using youth language practices to explore the importance of ethnic difference and interethnic unity; helping youth and communities to build coalitions both within and across difference. AAL was yet another example at South Vista of the ways young people in our changing communities and schools are living difference in new ways through language. AAL use and understanding at South Vista was one aspect of the rich linguistic dexterity and plurality of our young people. It joined Spanish, Samoan, Hindi, and Tongan in reinforcing and challenging lines of difference at South Vista. School must learn to use these resources to foster such complex togetherness in the face of a difficult, unequal, and increasingly multiethnic society.

Interlude: on oral language use, research, and teaching in multiethnic schools

The ways that languages were used and thought about in the youth space of South Vista were complex and multilayered. On one side were issues of ethnic solidarity and linguistic maintenance being played out every day inside and outside classrooms. The draw of solidarity and maintenance pushed youth to use cherished linguistic practices with others who shared their ethnic communities in South Vista and with others who shared memories of faraway homelands. Membership as a "Mexican" or a "Samoan" was tied up in linguistic abilities and was indexed in youth space, in homes, and in other community spaces to solidify and sustain social positionings.

With this push for in-group solidarity came the conscious and unconscious exclusion of out-group youth. For African Americans and Pacific Islanders, these exclusions through Spanish were too often filled with pain or frustration, reinforcing traditional lines of ethnic tension and division in difficult ways. At the same time, many youth struggled to come to terms with the knowledge that such in-group practices were necessary and understandable in the battle for marginalized identity maintenance. And these exclusions, however uncomfortable, also often kindled a desire to reach across difference to know and to understand the ways of others.

These desires to reach across difference were realized through language crossing and sharing, particularly in AAL and Spanish. Such practices of language across difference often brought youth together in marginalized solidarity, carving out youth identities set against broader dominant linguistic and cultural demands. Language crossing and sharing also worked to highlight linguistic desires and various levels of local prestige. While sustaining memberships in particular groups demanded language proficiencies, so, too, did sustaining membership in interethnic youth space. And so oral language use within and across ethnicity illustrated in bold social and cultural terms the workings of the paradox of pluralism. Both in-group solidarity and out-group sharing were needed to survive together in the face of the particular marginalization of heritage practices and in the face of collective marginalization as youth of color. Navigating the forces at work in this paradox required the development and use of various levels of linguistic dexterity. Ela had to be able to talk and comprehend AAL grammar and lexicon while simultaneously maintaining competence in Samoan. Miles needed to be able to retain his AAL prowess while working to find moments to share in Spanish. Julio needed to index his community membership through Spanish and his identity as a basketball player through AAL.

With these developed and developing linguistic skill sets came youth theories of culture and ethnicity that challenged easy definitions of us versus them. These ways of thinking among the youth in my work were the cognitive complement to the dexterous ways of acting. Where linguistic dexterity showed the agility to shift styles, varieties, and languages to claim identities in various domains, linguistic plurality showed the capacity to see language as a tool of both intraethnic and interethnic communication and identity. Linguistic plurality allowed youth to both share language and hold it dear; to give and to retain simultaneously.

Other scholars have recently begun to take up the call to explore the linguistic and cultural *contact zones* (Pratt, 1991) and *borderlands* (Anzaldúa, 1987) at the heart of multiethnic youth space. They have come up with other important ways to conceptualize the dexterity and plurality I came to understand at South Vista.[1] Yet this recent work is far from the dominant stream of scholarly inquiry into the linguistic and cultural experiences of marginalized young people. Rather, US educational linguistic research in general and social language and literacy research in particular remains monocular in its focus on ethnic in-groups. Our current research is segregated in ways many communities no longer are. To be clear, residential segregation maintaining division between communities of color and White communities is still the norm in the urban United States. But changing multiethnic communities like South Vista are also increasingly the norm. While we continue to need research by scholars skilled in the languages and cultures of particular groups, we also very much need research which inquires across language and ethnicity.

In fact, no research studies have focused on some of the key issues in Chapters 2, 3, and 4 despite the massive number of multi-ethnic schools in the United States. Youth understandings of the role of Spanish in multiethnic schools, the experiences and language struggles of Pacific Islander youth, and perspectives and uses of AAL in multiethnic schools and youth communities are little understood. And the specific processes of solidarity, exclusion, crossing and sharing through oral language in multiethnic youth space is equally understudied. Although my findings in these areas are far from exhaustive, I hope these chapters can open up research directions for others interested in understanding oral language and difference in multiethnic schools and youth communities in the United States and beyond.

TEACHING WITHIN AND ACROSS DIFFERENCE

The major educational implications of the oral language use and understanding of youth at South Vista are also considerable. An educational program which can work with the resources available along the continuum of linguistic solidarity, exclusion, crossing and sharing to capitalize on and extend the dexterity and pluralism of multi-ethnic space will require several key ingredients. I dedicate the final paragraphs of this interlude to laying out these factors of a pedagogy of pluralism.

Let me go about this discussion by taking on the role of a teacher developing a language and literacy curriculum for a classroom like those in South Vista. Theorists of pedagogy and curriculum have long argued that social and cognitive growth begins by posing relevant, engaging problems for learners to work through (Dewey, 1938; Freire, 1970; Tyler, 1949).[2] My listening and thinking with the youth of South Vista has revealed the issues of language use they most cherish, most want to extend, and those that cause them the most tension. Once relevant learning problems are found in collaboration with the learning community, these learning theorists prescribe overarching goals of learning, or outcomes, that a program intends to achieve. The primary goal in my classroom is to help youth explore, problematize, and extend their experiences and understandings of language as a tool of solidarity, exclusion, and unity. That is, youth should come away from this teaching and learning with a critical understanding of how and why language is used to challenge and reinforce difference and division, to exclude and to unite, and how they can participate more fully in making such social processes more positive and transparent for all members.

Now that I have an overarching goal and a set of relevant problems, I can go about designing learning experiences that will help youth work through the problems toward reaching this larger goal of critical language awareness and participation. The first set of experiences must bring the problems to the fore. This is the territory of journaling, of discussion, and of synthesis. In this early part of the program youth must be asked, as I asked them in our formal interviews, how they view the many ways with words they and others use in youth space. They should also, through journaling, fieldnotes, and audio recording, bring in examples of language use in their peer, home, and community domains. As the teacher I must also collect and observe to add to the educative material. I am now explicitly inviting Spanish, Samoan, Fijian, Hindi, and AAL into the classroom space for consideration.

With these materials in hand, it is time to guide youth through the major themes or categories of language use and understanding and the social reasons behind these major themes. The big themes from my research are likely to emerge in these discussions (as they did in my interviews and conversations with youth in South Vista) but, like any able teacher, I have them at the ready to throw out to the students as additional problems for consideration.[3] Discussions of solidarity, maintenance, exclusion, crossing, and sharing have now made it into our classroom. Yet we do not stop with raising the issues. We move further into what these issues mean to our identities as members of marginalized groups in historical context and in our present lives and possibilities.

Let me sketch out just a bit more. With some beginning consciousness in place around the big issues and what they mean to coexisting and to surviving as members of particular marginalized groups, it is time to get a little sociolinguistic. It is time to look at languages, their histories and their structures; it is time to do some learning of these languages and to learn about them. This is where student and teacher knowledge must coalesce. We take the language examples from the community and look at how they work and when they are used. Together, we contrast them with each other and, importantly, contrast them with DAE conventions. We look at the habitual be and talk about tense and aspect in AAL. We explore the youth lexicon, including the N-words, with an eye toward putting them in historical context, racialized context, and gendered context. We look to see if AAL is a "slang" and where its historical roots begin. Together we can investigate the basic syntax of Spanish to see if Rochelle was right in saying that "Spanish is like English only backwards." We do an inventory of the Spanish words and phrases non-Spanish speakers use and look to extend that repertoire, inviting the Spanish speakers to become conversational language teachers. We look at the history of Spanish in the United States and why it is and is not taught in schools. Samoan, Fijian, and Hindi come in as well. We think about pronunciation, about syntax, and get some elementary language lessons along the way. We think about why we don't often hear these languages. And all of this content is continually related back to the major issues of solidarity, exclusion, maintenance, sharing, and identity.

What has happened here? AAL, Samoan, Hindi, Fijian, and Spanish have entered our classroom space in the service of honoring heritage and identity and of working toward extending cultural and linguistic dexterity and pluralism. We are sharing the funds of knowledge, we are contrasting the ways of youth, and we are looking to take what they know and care about and using it as a critical resource. By bringing DAE into the discussion we have also allowed youth to grapple explicitly with issues of power and access rather than simply forcing DAE on them in an academic and intellectual vacuum.

The teacher knowledge about language and culture needed to implement such an educational program is considerable and will take redoubled efforts at language awareness in teacher education. It is important to note, though, that such efforts need not fall on one teacher alone. Rather, they should ideally be part of school-wide programs seeking to bring discussions of difference, division, and unity to the classroom. English teachers, biology teachers, and Spanish teachers should all be involved. Remember that the instances of crossing, sharing, and exclusion I have explored in these chapters happened between youth across a range of subjects and school and community spaces.

My musings here should provide ample material to consider the ways a critical language awareness curriculum might utilize the complex language issues at play in a pedagogy of pluralism. The bottom line is that we worry much about ethnic division and language development in schools, but give little chance for young people to grapple with these issues in the ways they live them. We do little with students to explore such vital facets of skill and self as language use. South Vista High, like most schools in the current standards and accountability era, was a case in point here, missing vital opportunities to adequately use the extraordinary language resources of the students and the community.

What is our goal in language learning in an increasingly multiethnic and multilingual society? What do we hope students know about and are able to do with language? Over my year at South Vista I came to know about the social goals of youth, about their language awareness, and about the ways they negotiated identity in a multi-ethnic and multilingual youth community. I came to know something of what they knew and were able to do with oral language. Their knowledge and ability was extraordinary. It challenged in fundamental ways what belonged to whom and when. It also illuminated pain and frustration and fear. "It's our culture, we have to," said Carlos about using his Spanish in youth space. "They're in my culture, they speak the same way," said Miles about his AAL in youth space. We have a long educational road to travel if we are going to honor culture and language in the ways Carlos, Miles, and all of their peers yearned for; if we are going to walk with them toward a dexterous and pluralist future.

5 "You rep what you're from": texting identities in multiethnic youth space

> DJANGO: Here you have "True Hamoz" (True Samoan). Tell me why you write the things down. Why do you write it on there? *(I point to the text Ela has written inside the commercial Superman logo on her backpack)*
>
> ELA: I don't know. I like writing stuff all over my backpack, you know, "Samoan."
>
> DJANGO: But why do you write "Samoan?"
>
> ELA: Because I love where I grew up at ...
>
> (March 15, 2007)

IDENTITY TEXTS AS AN ANALYTIC LENS

The youth of South Vista wrote texts on their backpacks, clothing, and skin. They sent texts from cellular phones and over online spaces. And many authored and performed texts as youth emcees. These texts pulsed through the everyday canvases of youth space defining who was a member of particular groups and who was not in a textual argument of solidarity, exclusion, crossing, and sharing. This textual argument mirrored through the written word the processes of oral language at South Vista. I came to understand these cultural inscriptions as *identity texts,* an analytic category that allowed me to parse out the workings of various types of text while seeing them also as a whole textual system. I use the term identity texts to refer to youth space texts inscribing ethnic, linguistic, local, and transnational affiliations on clothing, binders, backpacks, public spaces, rap lyrics, and electronic media. These texts were bound together by three factors: they indexed identities as members of particular groups, they were unsolicited literacy acts not officially evaluated by school, and all youth at South Vista participated in creating them.

I analyze three types of interconnected texts in this chapter. The first, *worn texts*, were those written on objects such as clothing and backpacks. The second were *delivered texts* and were sent and received via electronic media. I call original raps written and performed in youth space *flowed texts*. In looking at these three types of texting I join a long tradition in seeing all oral and written language as socially performed throughout.[1] Further than the socially performed activity of printing on paper texts, these identity texts engaged in a multimodal performativity that Lunsford (2007) has called *secondary literacy*. Such literacy spans various media between the oral and written, the textual and otherwise symbolic, the static word and the moving word, the dominant voice and the marginalized one.[2]

In attempting to understand the ways such identity texts resisted dominant systems and expectations of print at South Vista High, I find de Certeau's (1984) notion of the *scriptural economy* particularly helpful as a backdrop. De Certeau theorizes that the everyday power of "writing" (comprised of a blank space, a text, and a social purpose) has been subsumed by institutions (like schools and courts) and capitalist class structures to create and sustain the haves and have-nots. This economy functions through writing individuals and groups into being through systems of recorded text with clear, dominating social purposes. On the micro institutional level of South Vista High, such textual records include cumulative files of academic and social evaluation, report cards, and demographic summaries of race/ethnicity and language proficiency. De Certeau's scriptural economy also maintains its power by defining who is literate, educated, and potentially productive given the set of institutional records, thereby reinforcing classed (and I would add racialized and language-based) power inequities. I submit that in schools like South Vista, what counts as legitimate text, either at the institutional level or the individual level of student-produced writing, also participates in this economy as students' school writing is regulated, evaluated, and translated into the systems of power that determine their worth and advancement.

Set against this dominant scriptural economy was the *counter-scriptural economy* of youth space; the practices I am referring to as identity texts. In many crucial ways such texts resist and attempt to survive outside the dominant economy. Although such textual acts and counter economies in no way eclipse the power (and access) held by the dominant economy, I will offer evidence in my analysis that they hold important keys for re-visioning school writing, particularly for youth whose languages and cultures are marginalized.

Like the oral language practices I explored in the previous chapters, these identity texts fell along a continuum in multiethnic youth space. Some texts were primarily designed as markers of in-group solidarity and out-group exclusion. Other texts worked more to span ethnic and linguistic differences and create conditions of shared youth space. And still other texts found important middle ground by simultaneously forging in-group and cross-group identities.

As I observed and, at times, participated in this textual world of multiethnic youth space, the questions that echoed across all my work at South Vista came to rest on the counter-scriptural economy: how did these texts reinforce and challenge notions of ethnic and linguistic difference? How did these texts resist and offer alternatives to school-sanctioned writing?

"TRUE HAMOZ GURL FO LYPH": MAPPING CULTURAL GEOGRAPHY THROUGH WORN TEXTS

Texts covered the objects youth owned or attempted to own. Youth texted on walls, benches, binders, backpacks, clothing, and skin in economies of various scales. Some print was a global or national phenomenon. Clothing brand names like "Nike" and "Girbaud" and "Ecko" were etched boldly onto the delta force kicks, baggy multi-pocketed jeans, and over-sized T-shirts worn by the youth of South Vista. Such texts were examples of the large-scale commercial economy of print that gripped the imaginations and pocket books of youth and families across the nation and beyond.

Other print at South Vista was produced on a regional and metropolitan scale. Miles' T-shirt, "We Rep Tha Metro" or Rahul's locally painted T-shirt with the likeness of an infamous local bridge are examples of this metropolitan-scale text. Still other text was even more localized: a message quickly scrawled in permanent marker on the bathroom wall shouting "Cross-Town" or the local Norteño gang symbol "IVX," or Carlos's T-shirt, which proclaimed South Vista the "Little City Killing Zone."[3] These neighborhood- and city-scale texts indexed local geographic identities on personal and public objects. And finally there were even smaller-scale individual and in-group texts that worked to express various linguistic and ethnic identities.

It is at these regional, local, and individual scales that I analyze worn texts in the youth spaces of South Vista. This is not to minimize the larger economies of print at play in South Vista, across the nation, and globally. Such print certainly played an important role in identity as it enacted consumer culture. After all, upwards of 90 percent of the hundreds of female and male youth I observed inside and outside classrooms wore Nikes. Much important thinking should be done at this global-national scale, but my analysis here focuses on texts and symbols authored by youth and their local communities for youth and their local communities. I remain interested in the small acts of linguistic and literate agency because these acts provide, I think, an important key in remedying our perpetual educational failures around literacy for marginalized young people. That is, it is in looking at the texting that youth practice to affirm and create identities that I can most easily reflect on and revise the types of writing we so often demand of them in classrooms and society.

The significance of such local worn identity texts did not occur to me until early in the second semester as I sat in the back of Ela, Rahul, Rochelle, and Miles' biology class. I was in my customary seat taking my customary notes as students took theirs. I had observed this classroom weekly since September and, as I usually did, I scanned the walls and noted any changes to postings. As I looked around the room my eye fell on the collection of backpacks strewn anarchically in a pile a few feet behind me. Students were not allowed to have their backpacks with them at tables or desks, so

Figure 1 True Hamoz gurl fo lyph

this was also very usual. Ela's backpack, which I had been looking at for some weeks, came into hyper-focus in that moment. Figure 1 is the picture I took that day in the classroom. I have blurred out some identifying information.

Ela's backpack text is complex and multilayered, playing with symbol and language to index various identities. At the top of the text Ela created a feminist revision of the commercial Superman emblem, resisting traditional uses of the symbol by using the "S" to write "Superwymen."[4] In addition to her feminist statement, Ela also appropriated the "S" in the commercial emblem of Superman to write "Samoan Pride," a bold indexing of ethnic identity. She wrote "Samoan Pride" again on the right side of the text, this time in bamboo-style lettering characteristic of the Samoan tattoos she and her cousin planned to get on their next visit home to the island. Importantly, these two statements of ethnic pride and their feminist counterpart were written in English (versus Samoan) for all people who could read English at South Vista to understand. Also printed across the "S" is the local Hip Hop greeting "Wut it do do!" {How is it going?}, associated with the Metro Area music and dance movement known as "Hyphy."

Remembering this text was written on a backpack and was no more than 18 inches across, it takes even greater focus to see a further identity message. Ela inscribed the message "True Hamoz gurl fo lyph" {True Samoan girl for life} on the far right side of the emblem, communicating major elements of ethnic and linguistic solidarity with both her Samoan community and her broader youth community. This statement is particularly remarkable given the relatively infrequent use of Samoan at the school that I discussed in Chapter 3. Writing in Pacific Islander languages was even rarer at South Vista than spoken Pacific Islander languages. The majority of Ela's peers would not know what "Hamoz" {Samoan for "Samoan"} meant. Ela's use of "Hamoz" was a small act of agency, of linguistic pride against the general silencing of Samoan.

Another feature to notice in the text was the small phonological sharing in AAL by representing r-vocalization with "for" as "fo."⁵ Although the primary purpose of this backpack text was as solidarity with her Samoan community, Ela used AAL too, showing the ways in which such distinctions between solidarity and sharing at South Vista participated in the paradox of pluralism, falling on a continuum of practice rather than at opposing poles. Ela and the many youth who represented "for" as "fo" knew the conventional spelling but, in the counter-scriptural economy of identity texting, resistance to DAE norms was the standard. Continuing for a moment with the resistant orthography, Ela's spellings of "Superwymen," "gurl," and "lyph" are examples of eye dialect (alternative spelling that does not change the sound, but indexes vernacular language). The "ph" in "lyph" is particularly interesting as the now relatively mainstream word "phat" {nice, great} incorporated this spelling over a decade before my work in South Vista. In this way, using "ph" had become a popular counter spelling far beyond South Vista.⁶

Text was a central topic of my many formal and informal conversations with Ela over the year. This was, of course, in part due to my growing realization of the role of text in communicating identity, in drawing and redrawing lines of ethnic and linguistic difference. But it was also because Ela, like many students at South Vista, carried text with her both physically and, as well, in her imagination. Thinking about Ela's carrying of text on body and in mind will help further illuminate the significance of her backpack text and allow me to look into the broader world of worn text at South Vista.

Ela had a notebook full of her drawings and texts of various symbols and words of Samoaness. On March 5th, 2007, I interviewed Ela out on our customary bench between the school and the adjoining athletic field. She had brought her notebook that day and we leafed through it as we talked. In several previous conversations Ela had told me she planned to get large tattoos on her legs during her next trip to Samoa. A few times during the interview Ela used Samoan words or referenced them as they appeared in her notebook. By this time in the year I had received a few informal Samoan lessons from Ela, so I knew some of the words. I provide an extended excerpt of our conversation to try to understand the links between ethnicity, language, and imagined and real worn texts. I have added some descriptive transitions for clarity.

ELA: All night I've been thinking about a tattoo.

DJANGO: You've been thinking about it? Tell me what you'd get. Here, draw it. Can you draw what you'd get?

E: Hold up, let me think. Well, you know the Samoan name at the front of my binder? I want to write that one, and the flower.

D: Which Samoan name?

E: You know how I draw "Samoan" on my binder?

(Ela points to a large text stating "Samoan" drawn in bamboo-style lettering on her binder)

D: Here, let me see. Oh, yeah, the ones you were talking about for the tattoo. Who made these letters?

(She pushes the binder over toward me for a clearer view)

E: Me. Oh, I'm gonna get one – I think it's in my other – other notebook.

(Ela takes out another notebook, this one full of "Samoa" written in different styles and Samoan-style flowers. She shows me another "Samoa," this one next to a hibiscus flower she drew)

D: Let's see. Yeah, that's nice.

E: Then we got this one, "Samoan."

D: Oh, with the flower?

E: Yeah, we draw those – this one ...

(Ela points to another "Samoa" text, this one next to the word "alofa" [love])

D: That's nice ... And that means "love," right?

E: Yeah.

D: See, I'm learning ... And that's –

(I point to a word I do not know)

E: "Teine" in Samoan.

D: "One hundred percent Samoan ...?"

(I read the text without the last word, which I still do not know)

E: "Teine" means "girl" in Samoan.

There is a strong connection between the public messages Ela already texted on her personal objects, like her backpack and binder, and the messages she imagined inking permanently onto her skin. Imagining such permanent identity marks was a way of suggesting and projecting a stronger level of commitment to particular public identity messages. Ela had already made major public commitments by displaying messages of Samoaness and of resistant language on her personal objects, but for her and for other youth across ethnic groups at South Vista, tattoos were a next level of worn text which few had yet attained.

Ela's frequent imaginings of body language were not idle thoughts.[7] Many of the adults in her family, both men and women, had tattoos pronouncing ethnic and national pride, and tattoos are an accepted and common cultural practice in Samoan and, more broadly, in Polynesian cultures. Nor were other youth imaginings far from reality. Many young Latino/a and African American adults, both male and female, had tattoos ranging from family names, to gang symbols, to neighborhood affiliations.

There were striking differences in the types of messages the young people of South Vista wore on themselves and imagined wearing on their skin. These differences seemed to link most closely with ethnicity and, for Latino/a and Pacific Islander youth, with time-in-country. While Ela (who had arrived in the United States three years before my study) was inscribing messages of Samoaness and youth solidarity on her personal objects and was creating a notebook full of various styles of "Samoa" to get tattooed on her legs, Carlos and Miles had other thoughts of what was appropriate for inking versus what was appropriate for wearing on clothing and inscribing on binders and other spaces. In an early spring interview, Carlos drew strong lines between the identity texts on his objects and what he envisioned tattooing on himself. I have again included some clarifying information.

DJANGO: And then there's things that people write on their backpacks, and sometimes even tattoo or whatever.

CARLOS: Like 555?

(This was the city area code, often worn on clothing, hats, and written on backpacks, walls, and other objects)

D: Well yeah, so 555.

C: I think that's stupid, it's an area code, what the hell. Like my dad and I, we make fun of my cousin, because he got it tattooed right here. And my dad was like, "Okay, you might as well get your phone number." Like 555–638–2073, since you already have the area code. That's just retarded getting a tattoo of the area code of your city.

D: What other tattoos do people you know have?

C: "South Vista." I wouldn't – I mean, I like to represent it [by writing it on my personal objects] so they can see that I'm from there, but I wouldn't want to get it tattooed, it's just a city.

D: Right. Is there anything you would get tattooed?

C: Probably my parents' names ... if I got a tat it would have to mean a lot to me.

(March 12, 2007)

Unlike Ela, Carlos's imagined tattoos were not focused on ethnic pride, or even on his South Vista community, but rather were reserved for the names of family members. To be clear, Carlos, like all the youth in my work, participated heavily in worn texts. His worn text, however, centered on the regional and local scales of South Vista and the Metro area. They were texts that reached across ethnicity to claim unity with the larger youth community of South Vista. He explained why this was so during the same March interview.

DJANGO: Here, let me see your backpack. So you got "pretty girl" [his nickname for his girlfriend] and then you have "South Vista." What else you got on here? What is all this stuff?

(I search for the meaning of a massive graffiti-style text spanning his backpack)

CARLOS: That's all "South Vista", that's just "South Vista."

(Carlos points out the letters which slowly come into focus for me)

D: Oh, okay ... So tell me about – tell me about, like –

C: The tagging?

D: Yeah, why would you put it on your backpack?

C: I mean, I put it all over. I wear "Tha Metro" shirts and stuff, because I want to show people that even though I'm from South Vista I'm – like I'm smart and I can succeed ... Like when I went to [a school and non-profit sponsored trip to the American South] I purposely grabbed, like, all the shirts that said "South Vista," "Tha Metro," "555" because I wanted to prove to them that I was from Tha Metro, and I was from South Vista, and I was still smart. I could do anything that they could do, like, the other kids from any other city.

Carlos was clear here about his reasons for the sorts of identity texts he wrote on his objects and bought from local counter-economy clothing artists. He was wearing place to resist and dismantle what he felt were backward stereotypes that held him and his peers as less than. Carlos, who often spoke about his own navigations as a "smart gangster" – a kid who could both represent the community and do well in dominant society – saw his worn texts as a revolutionary act. Importantly, Carlos did not tag or wear "Mexico" or "Michoacán," even though he arrived in South Vista from Michoacán, Mexico in 1999. Although many more-recent Latino/a immigrants in Carlos's peer group did wear shirts and write messages of national and regional Mexican identities on their objects and on walls and benches, Carlos told me that he felt stronger about showing he was from South Vista than from Mexico.

Miles, much like Carlos, and like all of the African American youth I worked with and observed at South Vista, wore texts claiming neighborhood and metropolitan affiliations. Whereas Ela's worn texts focused on her ethnic, gender, and national identity and shared some in AAL and resistant orthography, and Carlos could choose to focus on worn texts of local affiliation and the youth lexicon versus other possible national and linguistic identities, African American students did not have these same options. As I explored in Chapter 4, AAL was the major choice of sustained oral language sharing, and this was true in identity texts as well. For Black youth, the city itself was the primary focus of worn texts. In the face of demographic changes, Miles and his African American peers seemed to use worn texts to claim that the city still belonged to them as much as anyone else. These texts were also a way to express a nuanced cultural geography of South Vista that gave meaning to space and place for all of the city's youth.

Such texts represented the most local scale in the economy of worn text and mapped out the neighborhoods of South Vista into three areas: "Central-Town" (or "C-Town), "Tha District," and "Tha Fields." Although all youth understood and texted these areas on a range of objects, it was African American youth who seemed to treasure, author, and preserve them most strongly in my observations. Miles explained these areas and their corresponding colors in the following interview excerpt. He also theorized about the scales of worn texts and identity claims, from local to regional.

> MILES: Tha District is red. Tha Fields has blue, and the C has green. So, you know, it's like your little own area. It's like Bronx and Brooklyn and Harlem and all that. But just on a very, very, very, very, tiny scale.
>
> DJANGO: That's interesting. And so you think of the C as kind of where you're from in terms of where you were born and where you grew up.
>
> M: Uh, huh.
>
> D: Do you think of South Vista that way or is it just the C?
>
> M: Inside of South Vista, I rep the C. Outside of South Vista – inside the Metro area, it's like South Vista, you know … And then outside of the Metro area to LA, it's like Tha Metro. But then it stops there. You don't really rep California.
>
> (March 26, 2007)

Miles "represented" or claimed geographic identity through the shirts he wore and through what he wrote on his objects, depending on his own physical proximity to home. These scales of texts and geographic identities rippled outward stopping, for him, at the metropolitan borders. Of course, for Ela, Carlos, and other immigrant students, the identity claims of worn texts reached across international borders as well. Also notice that Miles compared the neighborhoods of South Vista to several historically Black boroughs in New York City, suggesting the desire for geographical ownership; a harkening back to the African American majority population he had seen diminish during his lifetime. Figure 2 is the hooded sweatshirt Miles often wore to school and in the community. I have changed some personally identifying information.

Figure 2 C-Town Hustler

Miles' sweatshirt indexed his membership in a certain area of South Vista, the C-Town neighborhood where he was raised. As he told me in the same interview, "You rep what you're from" – a person represents or indexes their affiliations with space and place through worn text.

The text of the sweatshirt is important for me to interpret in detail as a piece of discourse communicating many layers of representing "what you're from." It calls out "C-Town Hustler," marking Miles as a young man who was "hustling," or working to make money and social capital. It is interesting that "hustler" is spelled with the final "r" fully realized versus the common AAL or Hip Hop phonology "hustla," possibly indicating that the text caters to an audience both within and beyond youth space. Below "hustler" is the area code of South Vista, a way of placing C-Town in urban space. The dice at the bottom of the shirt seem symbolic of a quest for material success, but also importantly represent the chance involved in a life in C-Town. At the bottom of the text, along the green banner, is a message that virtually summarizes the text as a whole: "Money, Power, Respect."

In a sense these three words captured the meaning of the entire counter-scriptural economy of South Vista youth. In Cintron's (1997) work on graffiti among Latino gangs, he calls such public texts "an intense need to acquire power and voice" (p. 186) in situations which offer little of either. Such was the case with worn identity texts, as well as other types of identity texts; they attempted to gain material, cultural, and social power and respect within situations of linguistic and ethnic marginalization by a dominant school and societal culture.

In an attempt to claim status, youth participated in various levels of commitment and permanence to the public identity messages they wore. At the deepest level of commitment was the tattoo, either real or imagined. Next were the boldly inscribed texts on personal objects, like Ela's backpack. Less personal and public commitment to a particular identity was required of the many messages of neighborhood, national, and gang affiliations which adorned bathroom walls and school benches, though youth often knew who had written such messages.

And within these various intersecting levels of commitment were the various intersecting scales of identity claims, from individual, to ethnic and linguistic, to city or regional. A given worn text or tapestry of texts communicated various memberships to other youth and, as such, reinforced particular lines of difference and division and cut across others. What is certain is that all the young people in my work read the world of such texts and navigated identities and personal networks along the borders they texted along youth space.

In Table 5, I map out the sorts of *text acts* or identity claims youth made through worn identity texts.[8] I am interested in charting the types of identities youth were attempting to achieve through uses of worn text. As well, I chart the geo-personal scales of such texts.

Table 5. *Claims and scales of worn identity text*

Identity claim	Text scale	Example
Metro area membership	Metro area	*We Rep Tha Metro*
South Vista membership	Local city	*Little City Killing Zone*
Neighborhood membership	Local neighborhood	*C-Town Hustler*
Ethnic group membership	Transnational	*True Hamoz Gurl Fo Lyph*

I should mention that worn texts were actively regulated by school rules and caring adults. Carlos, who wore shirts listing the youth lexicon from the larger Metro area, was asked by school officials to leave the shirts at home as they did not like the words they displayed or the red gang-affiliated color of the letters. Messages of neighborhood affiliation and national and ethnic pride written on walls and benches were painted over daily, along with other identity texts denoting gang membership. This is not to say that school did not have reason to regulate and to cover. Gang violence and conflicting conceptions of public versus private space were real at South Vista High and in the community. Yet, in my observations, such regulation was not done critically to engage youth in conversations about why the regulation was needed, nor did caring adults look to understand or utilize the power and voice that were articulated across worn texts as sites for classroom learning.

"WAS UP DIS CHELLE WAT U DOIN": AAL AND RESISTANCE IN DELIVERED TEXT

While youth were busy creating, purchasing, and navigating the network of worn texts, another type of identity text was silently circulating through the multiethnic youth space of South Vista. Texts delivered throughout the day and night over electronic media constituted a matrix of real literacy for real social purposes through which youth across ethnic groups indexed various identities. Simple messages planning meeting points or communicating a state of being flowed through delivered text. And deeper commitments also inhabited these texts. Friendship and love were often negotiated through texting over phones and online social networking sites like MySpace. And delivered text was practiced intensely within classroom walls as well. I observed hundreds of text exchanges over phones, over social networking sites, and via email during official classroom activities.

The world of delivered texts, then, was huge and I only glimpsed a fraction of it during my year. To date, research has yet to look into the particular ethnic and linguistic identities expressed through text messages, and it is here where I will focus my rather narrow analysis in this section. Specifically, I am interested in the ways AAL made its way into the delivered texts of youth across ethnic groups and, more broadly, the resistant and hyper-efficient orthography of such texting.

The delivered texts I analyze here come from hundreds of text exchanges I had with youth at South Vista over phones and the Internet.[9] These exchanges began in the middle of the year after significant layers of trust and relationship had grown between us. After observing the prominence of such text and with my growing awareness of the role of text in communicating ethnic and linguistic identity, I realized I needed some access to this matrix. Many of the male youth, like Miles, Rahul, Julio, and Carlos asked for my information to begin the exchanges. I had to ask female youth, like Rochelle, Carla, Gloria, and Ela if I could email, text, and visit their social networking sites. As a result, I had extended exchanges with all the young people I focused on during the year.[10]

Such exchanges, of course, are major indicators of rapport, as are the ways my text accommodated somewhat to theirs as I learned from them.[11] The fact that I was the text audience is also a limitation of this particular data. As a Black/White biracial adult male of color with some facility in Spanish who primarily spoke varieties of English during my time at South Vista, I was hardly an ideal youth audience. While more work should be done investigating youth-to-youth delivered text in multiethnic settings, I take the linguistic and ethnic identity marking in these texts as evidence of both the strength of such practices across audiences and as a display of the sorts of vernacular writing and speaking I was fortunate enough to be included in. This is, then, participant observation at its most participatory.

I begin with a brief text messaging exchange I had with Carlos on October 20th, 2007 about the success of his South Vista Soccer team (Carlos was a team captain). The team was having a remarkable season and I had planned to go to the soccer game against the arch rival, the private South Vista Preparatory High School. I was quite sick that day, so I texted Carlos before the game. Our exchange follows.

> DJANGO: Yo C ... Wuz gonna come to the game bt am sick ... gd luk tho ... beat SV Prep!
> CARLOS: *BoY* wE wOn 3–1.!! We ø uNdaFeatEd 2 *gAmEz*!!!!
> *(ø symbol added)*[12]

I began my text to Carlos with "Yo" a long-standing AAL term of greeting.[13] I also participated in eye dialect with "wuz" and "tho" and hyper-efficient orthography with "bt" and "gd." Carlos's reply came some two hours later, after the soccer game had finished. He began his text with the AAL term of endearment "Boy" (here meaning friend). Carlos had set his phone to alternate lower and upper case letters which, for me, added to the exclamatory mood. He also employed a bit of eye dialect with "gamez," a word he most certainly knew how to spell conventionally. Perhaps most striking was his omission of the copula (We ø undefeated), a grammatical feature of AAL which Carlos also employed in his everyday talk (see Chapter 4).

Ten days later, as the team headed toward the league title, I texted Carlos again. Here is an excerpt of our exchange.

DJANGO: Whn is the nxt game?
CARLOS: The semi final iz *diz* Thursday at 4pm. Here at *da* school
D: Dang, U r heroes!!!
C: I know! ... We ø *makin* history! ... We ø undefeated!! We ø north division *champz*. And now we ø *goen* 4 sections.
(ø symbol added)

This text again showed Carlos employing linguistic features of AAL in his writing as well as other acts of resistance to DAE writing conventions. Carlos texted the phonology of AAL into his phone with "diz" for "this" and "da" for "the."[14] He also shared in AAL grammar by deleting the copula in a string of emphatic statements beginning with "We ø makin history!" Finally, Carlos represented "going" as "goen" and "making" as "makin," another common phonological feature of AAL and other non-dominant Englishes.[15] Also important are the features of eye dialect with "iz" and "champz," again resisting dominant conventions in words Carlos knew how to spell conventionally.

This grammatical sharing in AAL shows a close relationship between vernacular talk and text messaging that goes far beyond a mere efficiency of print and even beyond resistant orthography. Carlos was being a particular user of language here, was indexing a youth identity through uses of AAL and eye dialect. Crucially, these uses mirrored the identities Carlos expressed in the worn identity texts that adorned his personal objects and clothing.

Carlos and other Latino/a and Pacific Islander youth shared in AAL in delivered text, challenging lines of linguistic ownership and difference, joining their Black peers in texting as they joined them in their everyday talk.[16] African American students like Rochelle and Miles also participated heavily in the use of AAL features in delivered texting. Although this may not seem surprising, the types of features used and the fact they occur in writing *is* surprising. Representing the vernacular in writing is a more conscious act than the often unconscious act of using vernacular in speech, particularly when authors are writing words and constructions they use and know well in DAE. I will use a series of delivered texts I exchanged with Rochelle during the summer of 2007 to examine the types of AAL features that made their way into her and other African American youth texts at South Vista.

As our relationships strengthened over the year, I learned many wonderful things and difficult things about the youth I worked most closely with. And I believe firmly that ethnography and humanizing research is a two-way street, a dialogic activity much like teaching and learning. So I shared more details about my own life with the young people as the second semester progressed. One thing I learned about Rochelle was that she loved sunflowers. In a conversation one day I mentioned that my wife, Rae, planted dozens of sunflowers every spring. Rochelle was taken by this, so I brought some pictures of our previous year's crop. In the photographs, eight-foot Mammoths, multicolored Autumns, pastel Lemon Queens, and ruby-red Velvet Queens towered over our backyard fence. Rochelle most liked the Autumns; sunflowers with multiple red and yellow colored flowers that branch out like trees. I asked Rochelle if she'd like Rae to plant her some during the spring. I could bring them over to her house when they got big enough in the early summer. I rarely saw Rochelle smile as deeply as she did while saying yes.

Three months later I brought the seedlings over to Rochelle's house, a small home in the Cross-Town neighborhood of South Vista. It was June 22nd, 2007, and school had been out a week. When I arrived I noticed a potted garden lining the walkway to the front door. A dozen or so pots were home to white and pink roses, a few yellow Five O'clocks, a grapevine, and various other flowers and small trees. The plants were well cared for, but a bit withered and root bound. I asked Rochelle if we could put the seedlings in the ground near the chain-link fence. She said no, they needed to go in a pot like the other plants.

Later, while Rochelle and I were planting the seedlings in a large pot, her mother came out on the porch. We talked then, Rochelle's mother and me, about their situation. She told me she had all the plants in pots because they might have to move again. She did not want to move again after just a few months in this house. "I'm tired of moving, I just want a place to have a little garden, a place to be," she said. It felt like she was talking to me and to the sky. I thought of Mama's house plant in *The Raisin in the Sun* (Hansberry, 1959), symbolic of hanging on to life and hope in the face of economic struggle and racial injustice.[17] I was overwhelmed as I watched Rochelle give the seedlings their first water in their new home, so much so that I have returned to this scene many times over the years of analysis and writing since that day. And I will return once more to the larger significance of that day for understanding the nexus of pluralism, justice, and schooling in the concluding chapter of this book.

A week later I was sitting on the couch with Rae watching TV when Rochelle delivered this text, complete with the photograph in Figure 3. Our exchange follows.

Rochelle had delivered a picture of the sunflowers in their pot, a few inches bigger now, basking in the summer sun, with the text "Ma plants go.". Our exchange continued a bit.

DJANGO: They look nice chelle
ROCHELLE: I knw dj *tanx*

Rochelle's initial text was deeply significant on levels in addition to linguistic and ethnic identity. Her text was representative of our growing friendship and of her happiness at the state of her sunflowers. Note the nicknames "chelle," the name she told me she would rap and sing under, and "dj," the first two letters of my name. It is a reminder of the many levels of communication that flowed through the texting of youth space.

Figure 3 Ma plants go

On the linguistic level, Rochelle's delivered text shows several important features that indexed her identity as an AAL and youth lexicon speaker and writer. Texting "Ma" instead of "My" was an example of monopthongization, or the transformation of the two-vowel sound sequence in "My" (m-ah-ee) to a long one vowel sequence in "Ma" (m-ah).[18] Another phonological feature in the texts is "thanks" as "tanx,"[19] a voiceless consonant replacement even more common in Caribbean Creole varieties. Rochelle also used the local adjective "go" (something in a state of looking, sounding, or being good) common among youth of color in the larger Metro Area. Table 6 illustrates the AAL features in the text messages I exchanged with South Vista youth.

Cherished selves as members of the youth community of South Vista and the Metro area were forged and sustained through the linguistic choices youth made in delivered texting. For some, like Carlos, this meant crossing certain boundaries of linguistic division. For others, like Rochelle, media texting was a space to solidify

Table 6. *AAL features in text messages*

Feature	Example
Phonology	
Monopthongization	ma {my}
Consonant replacements	ing to in (ŋ to n): goin, doin~th to d
	(ð to d): da {the}, diz {this}
	Th to t (θ to t): tanx {thanks}
R and L vocalization	fo sho {for sure}, skoo {school}
Lexicon	Ducez {a salutation meaning
	"peace"}
	Hella {local adjective for
	"extremely"}
	Hatr {a person lacking respect}
Grammar	
Zero copula	we ø da champz
Regularized agreement	the tickets *is* 10
Immediate future tense markers	We *Fnah* {getting ready to} graduate
	Ima leave {I'm going to leave}

her position and prowess as an AAL and youth language user. For all youth at South Vista, delivered texting was a space where DAE norms and the evaluative eye of caring educators did not constrain why, what, how, or when they wrote.[20]

"A NEW ROOT": FLOWS IN SOUTH VISTA AND RAHUL'S TEXTUAL PLURALITY

Many of the young men I came to know at South Vista participated in writing and performing rap. Although young women participated heavily in Hip Hop culture through clothing, language, singing, and dance, in my observations they were less involved in the production of rap lyrics. This follows the trend of the larger national and global rap culture where female rappers are far outnumbered by their male counterparts. This is not, of course, to say that many women rappers have not contributed historically and do not continue to contribute deeply to the form, but that the vast majority of the rappers listened to by the youth in my study were male. In my observations and discussions with youth, gender participation in writing rap lyrics at South Vista was certainly reproducing the dominant gender lines of commercial Hip Hop culture.

Carlos, C.C., Jamal, Rahul, Terrence, and many others I knew wrote raps (known as "flows"), sharing them on the playground, through recordings, over electronic media, in battles, and even in the classroom as fully embodied counter scripts to official classroom literacy activities. Such flowed texts were shared across ethnicity, making a practice originating in African American and Caribbean American culture a major activity of the Latino/a and Pacific Islander youth communities of South Vista.[21] Before turning to a deeper analysis of the flowed texts themselves, I think it is important to show how these literacy practices made their way into the classroom space despite being actively uninvited. This will give some sense of the pervasiveness of flowed texts among young men at South Vista. Two brief fieldnotes give some indication of flowed texts in classroom spaces. The first fieldnote occurred in the eleventh grade humanities class I visited regularly.

The teacher is leading students through writing answers to a series of questions about Sinclair's *The Jungle*. I look over at Jamal, who is quiet and madly scribbling something on a paper. "What are you writing?" I whisper.

Jamal, "Something for work."

"A flow?" I ask. I know he and several other boys are part of a local arts program that pays them to rap at a studio. Two of the boys are on the basketball team.

Jamal, "How did you know?"

"I know what you do," I say with a smile.

Several minutes later students are still working on the questions and reading. Jamal passes me the rap. I ignore him and

look at the teacher, wait for her to look away then I take the rap.
It is mainly a boasting affair, full of references to "stunners"
(large sunglasses), gold chains, and "whips" (hyped cars). He also
mentions C-town and South Vista in the lyrics. As I read, Jamal
pounds his fist and stomps his feet quietly, giving me the back-
beat to the song.

(February 12, 2007)

It is difficult to miss the double irony of Jamal's counter-literacy practices. First, his literacy was set against the other classroom literacy –
the answering of literature questions – being officially prescribed
by the teacher. Second, Jamal's literacy was paying him, a minor,
for work while the class investigated Upton Sinclair's (1906) classic
novel about labor among oppressed working poor Americans. Beyond
these ironies, though, was the way Jamal attempted to embody his
texts with movement and sound as I read. He was in a powerful way
fighting against the more traditional print writing of the classroom,
trying to show the movement and performative aspects of flowed
texts. This practice of pounding out beats and spitting flows was
very common in classrooms. Here is another example from the same
class, this time in the library on December 13th, 2006. I was roaming
around and jotting notes when I came to a table with C.C., Carlos,
and two Latinas, Paola and Julissa, who I knew less well. The two
young men were getting down, rhyming and pounding away in the
midst of the library research going on around them. The two young
women were bobbing their heads to the beat as they worked.

I wander behind C.C. to listen as Carlos is making a beat on the
table to accompany C.C.'s rapping – "boom, boom, clack, boom,
boom, clack." When I get directly behind C.C. he flows, "Tall ass
nigga behind me" in rhythm as a lyric. The entire table laughs
and looks at me to see if I heard.

I tell the table, "I made it in to his rap" with a smile. "I'ma be
famous."

C.C. agrees and nods his head, "Yup, famous."

C.C. and Carlos, like Jamal, were embodying flows in all their multimodal grandeur, again part of a counter-scriptural economy set against the backdrop of the official classroom writing activities. These examples illustrate how classrooms, set up as spaces for particular types of behaviors and literacies, could not always hold flowed texts and their accompanying beats at bay. I asked Carlos about this in our March interview.

> DJANGO: Class will be going on, right, and then suddenly you'll hear, like –
>
> CARLOS: You'll hear a beat.
>
> D: You know, so you'll hear some beats. So tell me about –
>
> C: I don't know – it's part of our culture, like, South Vista. When you go to another city and you tell them, "Oh, South Vista, they like to go Hyphy."[22] They relate it to music instantly, because there's a lot of rappers in South Vista, in the Metro. And it's in us, like, music. We're bored, we don't have anything to do, we just start busting beats. And you don't even notice it … The teacher's all like, "Stop." And then I'm like, "Oh, I was just busting a beat and I didn't even notice." You don't say that, but you think about it. You don't even know when it happens, it's just part of our culture; it's who we are. I don't really think teachers understand that.
>
> (March 12, 2007)

Carlos saw the practice of making rhythms and rhymes in class as a way to occupy minds in the face of boredom. He added an important element of cultural solidarity, too, suggesting that such practices were "our culture," cutting across the landscape of ethnicity and language differences at South Vista. Whether or not such practices did, in fact, "distract the class," is less the issue here than the fact that they were in tension with official scripts. However, it was teachers, not students, who felt and acted on this tension most strongly.

Even though flowed texts did make their way into academic spaces, classrooms were by and large hostile places to make and perform flows. Crafting flows happened most densely in other, less regulated areas of multiethnic youth space. In the remainder of this section, I will analyze rap lyrics written and performed by Rahul, whose emcee name was Larul. Larul will serve as a case study of the types of identities texted through flows, and particularly for those claimed by Pacific Islander and Latino youth who might not traditionally be seen as valid emcees. I will show Larul's texts as examples of *textual plurality*; texts that reached both ends of the continuum of multiethnic youth space at once: texts challenging notions of difference even as they called out solidarity with particular groups.

The first example is an excerpt from a flow Rahul originally performed for me and his African American friend Dominique after biology class in mid-December. Like other youth rappers, Rahul always wrote his lyrics down before performing them. He gave me these typed lyrics a couple weeks after his impromptu performance.[23]

> They call me Rahul but pronounce Larul
> 'Cause I'm the one with the most *hustle loot*
> It doesn't run in my family so I call it *a new root* ...
> Yup keeping it real from south vista, *the metro, the yetro, mane,*
> From the *californ I A*
> From the *Fiji Islands* to this ghetto beautiful place
> I rose from *the streets*
> Teaching me to *kill it* on a type of beat
> From rock to country to Hip Hop to rap
> Yeah you know me as the *first Fijian* to ever do that

Larul's flowed text shows many features common to the raps I read and heard throughout the multiethnic youth space of South Vista. First, he shared in AAL and Hip Hop lexicon with the items "hustle loot" (street-made money), "the streets" (the urban community), and "kill it" (to do something well). His writing also employed a popular local Hip Hop and AAL pronunciation of "man" /man/ as "mane" /māne/. These are important textual representations of sharing in AAL and Hip Hop culture.

Rahul was, of course, aware that the language and cultural practice of his text did not stem from his Fijian heritage. As he put it, rapping was a "new root" and he was "the first Fijian." Instead, his flowed text tells us this craft came to him from "south vista" and "the metro" (which is repeated as the popular local Hip Hop derivative, "the yetro"). At the same time, by calling out "Fijian" he sought to maintain solidarity with his community that he might risk leaving behind by becoming a rapper. Finally, Rahul participated here in the larger AAL rhetorical tradition of toasting, declaring his imagined wealth and his prowess at the craft of flowing.[24]

Rahul's text was hardly as static as it appears here on the printed page. While the identity texts delivered through phones and Internet sites were in constant, building conversation, and the identity texts worn by youth were selected on particular occasions and often layered upon over time, flowed texts were usually shared aloud and recorded. In fact, the performed version of Larul's lyrics was flowed over the instrumental of a popular club song of 2006, The Game featuring 50 Cent's *How We Do* (2005). The lyrics to the original song detail the exploits of men driving flashy rides, toting hand guns, and making sexual advances on women in a dance club. Here are a couple of representative lines from The Game's original, which played non-stop on local airways for several months:

> These G-Unit girls just wanna have, fun
> Coke and rum
> Got weed on the ton
> I'm bangin with my hand up her dress like, unh

Rahul's version offered a rather revolutionary revision, focusing instead on what he termed "the real" topics of life in South Vista: ethnic pride, cultural sharing, and survival through lyrical expression.

Writing and recording raps, their meanings, and what they meant to a possible future for Rahul was a topic that dominated many of our interviews and conversations. And much of this talk focused on his multiple identities as a Fijian, a Hip Hopper, and a member of the local South Vista youth community. It is worth exploring Rahul's explanation of his lyrics for the *New Root* flow in thinking about these multiple selves as indexed through flowed text.

> DJANGO: And so tell me a little bit about the words to that flow.
>
> RAHUL: I wrote like, "From the Fiji Islands to this ghetto beautiful place." I came from the Islands, you know, and I'm doing it big right here. Someday you'll see us Fijian people rapping, you know, because most of your rapping people do it's like Mexicans and Blacks and stuff. Some Whites, but not a lot. And I'm trying to bring the Fijians out, trying to show what we got. Any of us Polynesians, you know ... No matter what race you are, what other people say, "Oh, you this race, you can't rap." No, if you got flows, you can rap ... When I'm saying "from the Fiji Islands'" it's not only indicating me, it's indicating my people from the Fiji Islands, you know? They come from there to this ghetto beautiful place, doing it big, so that's the thing. It's like an inspiration, so it's like a little direction to tell them how to go, where to go.
>
> (December 8, 2006)

Rahul's explanation touched importantly on the way his text, typed into his computer, rapped on the school yard, and recorded on a demo CD, claimed several identities at once. His lyrics embody a sort of triple purpose, showing his membership in South Vista, claiming prowess and acceptance as an emcee, and displaying solidarity with his Fijian community both in the United States and in Fiji. He was conscious of the many tensions he had to navigate to successfully claim these various memberships. Tensions over who can be a rapper and how his community continually adjusts to "doing it big" in new lands. The fact that Rahul had never traveled to his parents' homeland and that he was born and raised in South Vista did little to temper the intensity of his sense of Fijianess. Likewise, the fact that people said a Fijian shouldn't be rapping only fueled his drive to create flowed texts. On the level of broad themes, then, Rahul's flows showed a *textual plurality*, an ability to span difference and division, while at the same time challenging and embodying both of them.

The following song, *Fijian Coming Through*, further exhibits Rahul's use of AAL grammar and Hip Hop and youth lexicon in addition to the larger thematic identity claims. It was delivered to me over email in mid-June, 2007.[25] I have excerpted a few representative sections for analysis, preserving the opening and closing lines.

Fijian Coming Through
Im riding spider 22's
Ya niggaz aint even got a dam clue
Who ø coming, it's the *fijian, fijian* coming through ...
I can *spit* some with his or her name
Ya niggaz know *ima* wait till *ima* in the hall of fame
Yeah its coming, yeah *dats* me
Son coming ohhhh *besta believe* ...

My *flows* are *illmatic*
People known me as the rhyming kid fanatic ...
I'm not stating im better than *ya*
u give me some *props* im from the *metro area*
thats where I got my *ghetto routes*
ooh *ya* gonna know what im talking about

I *ain't* just running my mouth
I got *bling* from north to south ...

Cause *them niggaz* couldn't back *them* words up
If I were them I would just shut the fuck up
Or back my words up
got *bitches* that suck me like yummy caramel
In my city im liked real well
Not for *my game* but just me
Im one of kind
Cause you can't find unique laruls all the time

Better yet you can't find laruls
Im the only one, cause im the start of the root

Like so many of the flowed texts I read and heard in the youth space of South Vista, *Fijian Coming Through* is laden with linguistic and thematic elements claiming various identities across ethnicity, geography, and language. Among several other features of AAL phonology and grammar I have analyzed in previous texts throughout this chapter, Larul used the morphologically transformed "ima" for "I am going to" to reference a first person future action. Rahul was consciously concerned that his written representations were phonetically accurate. Choices like "ya" instead of "you" were deliberate, a point Rahul made to me on the yard in March 2007. He asked me if what I heard in the recordings matched what he had written and told me of how hard he worked to try to spell things like they sounded. His point was large and linguistic; it speaks to how our alphabet fails in so many ways and shows how Rahul actively resisted DAE spelling and phonology in his flows, mirroring the resistance found in other identity texts of South Vista.

Lexically, his flow contains the Hip Hop terms "illmatic" (extremely good), "props" (compliments), and the now mainstream "bling" (jewelry or other luxurious objects). The terms "niggaz"[26] and "bitches" were also employed by Rahul. Although his raps generally did not contain explicit scenes of sex or female exploitation and subjugation, this one certainly does. As part of the larger toasting scheme of the flow, Rahul included a boast about his (imagined) sexual prowess and control over "bitches." Mainstream commercial rap, as evidenced by the lines in The Game's song earlier in this chapter, is heavy with such objectification and oppressive sexual scenes.[27] As part of that culture, Rahul saw the need to include it.

I had some critical discussions about the terms "bitches" and "hos" with Carlos, Rahul, and Miles, all of whom said they realized their common terms for women were, as Carlos put it, "a lot negative." These young men were in a constant struggle to define womanhood and manhood in the face of conflicting feelings, messages, and semantics.[28] They were grappling with the cultural politics of how they would represent themselves and the young women in their communities, and how they as young men wished to be represented. School, of course, is in an ideal position to help youth develop critical understandings of gender and sexuality past simply regulating controversial and derogatory terms as off limits. The N-words and the B-words, for example, were simply made taboo with little discussion of why.

Membership in the larger Metro Area was also an important component of Larul's flow, with "u give me some *props* im from the *metro area* / thats where I got my *ghetto routes*." It is the final line of the song that completes the plurality involved in Rahul's flow. As he did in other songs, he called out his role as "the only one" and "the start of the root." He was once again explicitly stating that his participation as an emcee in Hip Hop culture was something new to his family and to his generation of urban Fijian American youth. The various ways he shared in linguistic and cultural practices to show who he was and what he cared about, then, were new paths he felt he was forging. They were paths that at once sought unified interethnic ground and maintained divisions of ethnic pride. Look out, he warned, "fijian coming through."

Like the other types of identity texts, linguistic elements were micro acts of identity layered on top of other macro-level content displaying ethnic, geographic, and linguistic identities.[29] Also like other forms of texts, major sharings occurred, cutting through particular borders of difference and reinforcing or drawing others. What was most intriguing about Rahul's flows were the way they exhibited a textual plurality, allowing him to index and embody membership in many communities at once. As he told me one time about his multiethnic peer group and various linguistic and cultural practices, "I wouldn't have it any other way."

The ways that the division between writing and oral performance were blurred in the flowed texts of South Vista also have important implications for classroom learning. Like worn and delivered texts, elements of vernacular talk made their way into flowed texts, often as explicit choices of resistance to dominant norms. Yet flowed texts in particular were often textual representations of what had already been or would be orally practiced or performed. Flowed texts, then, were attempts at capturing embodied orality in written form. This brings to mind discussions in new literacy studies of the false overarching separation between literacy and orality, and how such distinctions are historically and culturally determined.[30] The line between spoken and written for emcees was not always clear. We often separate written tasks from oral ones as if they have little relation, but capitalizing on the performed and oral nature of flows in classroom activities has the potential to promote elements of voice and style in both prose and public speaking.[31]

While so many South Vista youth were participating in flowed identity texts inside and outside the classroom, other important ways with text were being modeled and practiced by dedicated teachers inside the classroom. Yet the many possible bridges between flowed identity texts and traditional classroom texts were not part of the classroom lessons I observed. The utility of using rap in critical ways as a resource for classroom learning is quickly amassing.[32] It is high time such approaches gained wider application.

It is also important to realize that the exploding body of scholarship on rap, Hip Hop Nation Language, and Hip Hop culture remains, for good reasons, largely focused on African American produced rap and language. Hip Hop, of course, was born in African American and Caribbean American urban culture and the majority of US emcees remain Black. Yet, as Rahul and many others at South Vista and in urban communities across the nation and world show, we need to also look at the ways other groups in urban communities are participating deeply in flowed texts and the broader Hip Hop culture.[33]

Far beyond my romanticizing rap in general, or seeing it as the holy grail of urban literacy, is the simple fact that many young men of color, who continue to lead drop-out and incarceration rates, participate heavily in flowed texting. C.C. had dropped out of school by January, Rahul had to repeat classes he failed during the 2006–07 school year, and many other young men I knew were teetering on the brink of school failure. And yet literate selves pulsed through their flows in powerful ways that can teach us about the ways language, literacy, and ethnicity work among youth in multiethnic space: and about the new literacy attempting to claim and shape power, voice, and style. Who among us, the researchers and teachers of Englishes, of languages, of literacies, are ready for a level dialogue? In the conclusion to this chapter I explore the lessons of identity texts for teaching and learning in multiethnic urban high schools and imagine such a level dialogue between classrooms and the students they serve.

JOINING THE WORK OF THE COUNTER-SCRIPTURAL ECONOMY

The young people of South Vista were engaged in powerful literacy and identity work to claim ethnic, linguistic, and geographic affiliations, to share in AAL and Hip Hop culture across ethnic lines, to consciously resist DAE spelling and grammar, and to forge spaces for multimodal writing that were not often offered in the classroom. Like all writing, the identity texting of the youth I worked with at South Vista was intended to communicate meaning to audiences. In fact, the real social purposes of such texts had immediate meaning often more vital to youth than many of the official writing tasks students were asked to complete throughout their school days. This is in no way to privilege youth identity texts over other, dominant forms of writing necessary for broader access in dominant society. Simply celebrating and understanding the considerable cultural and linguistic ingenuity at work in these texts is a privilege we cannot afford. Rather, I make this point because such writing saturated the multiethnic youth space of South Vista and it offers an incredible, evolving resource for teachers and for the youth of color our schools continue to fail in brutally large numbers.

In my hundreds of hours of observation at South Vista I did not see worn, delivered, or flowed texts brought critically into classroom work, just as I did not see the oral language of youth space used critically in classrooms. The qualified and dedicated teachers of South Vista, working within district, state, and federal frameworks, of course, had many constraints upon the curriculum and pedagogy they were charged to employ. These external demands were by and large in line with the dominant, White middle-class values, behaviors, language, and literacies decades of researchers have shown at the center of US public school learning. Such monocultural demands go hand in hand with larger schemes of power and privilege that seek to maintain schools as mainstreaming institutions, particularly for those young people whose languages and cultures fall outside the dominant ways. The goal of such schemes, still laden with deficit thinking, is to transition youth like those in South Vista into dominant ways of being with little regard for linguistic or cultural maintenance. But this goal has hardly worked for masses of young people of color in US schools. Furthermore, what is lost in such a transition from locally prestigious practices to dominant ones? What sorts of oral and written language are silenced and suppressed? It seems to me, that by silencing the linguistic and textual economy of multiethnic youth space we are silencing knowledge about language, literacy, and plurality the United States has sought in word, if not in deed, throughout its history. That is, we are silencing keys to understanding the complex nexus of difference, division, unity, and the oral and written word.

Acknowledging the *culture of power* students need access to, while also acknowledging the *counterculture of power* marginalized youth participate in, will mean finding ways to join the work of youth texts and the work of dominant school texts to show the value of each for communicating meaning to and exercising power with audiences.[34] Building off Bhabha (1994), Gutiérrez *et al.* (1999) and her collaborators have called such a joining of official school practices and knowledge with the unofficial youth practices and knowledge the *pedagogical third* space.[35] Gutiérrez (2008) has strengthened this concept by calling for educators to move beyond simple resource models that take marginalized practices as mere bridges to more important dominant ones. She argues we need teachers and youth to collaborate on understanding each other's languages, literacies, and cultures in this third space where new, hybrid practices will emerge.[36] What must we do to bring the work of identity texts into level dialogue with more traditional school print literacies?

First, we must acknowledge that *new rhetorics*[37] and literacies are evolving to include sounds, voices, language varieties, and organizational structures that school writing has been unable and unwilling to deal with. This was certainly the case at South Vista, where school writing was mainly a print on page, standard essay affair. It is somewhat telling that I needed photographs to analyze worn identity texts and would need audio to do analytic justice to flowed texts. Joining the work of identity texts means that teachers must stretch traditional school genres to include the sorts of media, modes, and performativity demanded in youth space and in many workplaces and professions. Schools must work to incorporate worn, delivered, flowed, and many other types of multimodal and digital literacies into classroom lessons.

In addition to revising what text and writing can encompass, pedagogy needs to address the many levels of ethnic and youth identity as well as resistance to DAE norms evident at the linguistic levels of syntax, phonology, morphology, and lexicon. While important work has looked at the way AAL grammar and organizational patterns carry into the writing of AAL-speaking students,[38] research has not looked at conscious carry-over in the textual economy of youth space, nor at such features among Latino/a youth, Pacific Islander youth, and youth of other backgrounds. Yet, as I referenced in Chapter 4, we know much about pedagogical and curricular strategies to support youth in using AAL literacy practices while acquiring DAE literacy practices.[39] To truly join youth texts, such strategies must also engage in critical conversations about power and audience and history – the "why" behind a need to acquire command of multiple written and oral varieties. In addition, educators need to be willing and able to see such linguistic features in text as valid, equal modes of communication.

Through worn, delivered, and performed texts, the youth of South Vista communicated who was with them and who was not in a textual argument mapping out their pluralistic reality. To genuinely *problem pose* using the purpose and power of such texts as a foundation will begin to forge a third space that invites the counter-scriptural economy of youth texting into dialogue with the dominant one that the school promotes and demands.[40] In the process, both youth and their teachers will need to grapple with the ways that claiming difference and reinforcing division through text *and*, at times, cutting across those differences and divisions is what makes shared cultural spaces possible and productive. Ela's statement of her Samoaness inscribed on her backpack, Rochelle's and Carlos's expressions of AAL and youth language in their text messages, and Rahul's flows blending his Fijian and emcee identities show youth employing print and other literacies to at once challenge and reinforce traditional notions of difference and notions of writing. It is our job as researchers and educators to learn to read these texts and meaningfully incorporate them into classroom lessons about audience, purpose, grammars, difference, and power.

Finally, to enter a third space we need to access the larger frameworks of solidarity, exclusion, crossing, and sharing evident in oral language use, which identity texts also participated in through genre and thematic content, through linguistic features, through explicit ethnic and gender identity claims, and through the expression of various scales of geographic identities. Such a social study of writing and reading focused on the complex web of identity texting as it relates importantly to school literacy and power necessarily complicates the notions of difference, division, and unity at the heart of this book. And it necessarily joins the stance to teaching within and across difference that defines the pedagogy of pluralism.

The youth of South Vista were engaged in a textual dexterity that shows great promise for what education can and must do to reinvigorate language and literacy learning in multiethnic high schools where youth are engaged in living and writing together in difference. The longer I looked and listened to these texts, the more I heard youth calling out to each other, to me, and to all those genuinely interested in listening. Miles' C-Town sweatshirt demanded, "Money, Power, Respect." If we are honest, we all need a little of each; and so do our young people. We can begin by trying to understand the textual worlds they create and live within.

6 Making school *go*: re-visioning school for pluralism

> We are in the middle of an extraordinary social experiment: the attempt to provide education for all members of a vast pluralistic democracy. To have any prayer of success, we'll need ... a philosophy of language and literacy that affirms the diverse sources of linguistic competence and deepens our understanding of the ways class and culture blind us to the richness of those sources.
>
> Mike Rose, *Lives on the Boundary*

A vast question loomed over all of my learning with the youth of South Vista, as it now looms over the closing chapter of this book: what is the purpose of schooling in a pluralist society? The history of schooling in the United States, a country home to epic linguistic, racial, and cultural diversity, has traditionally defined this purpose rather clearly. The purpose of schooling has been to transition or mainstream the ways of knowing and being of those whose cultures and languages fall outside the dominant stream into White, DAE, middle-class norms. Yet volumes of research and theorizing in the past three decades have profoundly challenged these narrow assimilatory goals.[1] This work has critiqued both the unsatisfactory academic results for young people of color and the perpetuation of racial and cultural bias through assimilatory models of education.

As we enter the second decade of the twenty-first century, we are presented with an exceptional opportunity to push for the possibilities of linguistic and cultural equanimity espoused in the early days of the United States and continued in contemporary rhetorics of social justice.[2] Our demographics are changing and our schools are changing with them. The shifting demographics of communities and schools like South Vista offer an amazing chance to re-vision language, literacy, and humanities education in ways that utilize the dexterity and plurality in the practices and minds of young people.

In truth, schools have always been ideal sites to support and foster such cultural and linguistic dexterity and plurality, though they have not historically done so. With so many urban (and, increasingly, suburban and rural) US public schools now serving multilingual and multiethnic communities, we must reassess our traditional notions of difference even as we strive to respect and maintain the cultural and linguistic practices so cherished by communities. This is the ground of the *pedagogy of pluralism*, a pedagogical stance whose practices I have attempted to sketch out at the conclusion of each of the chapters.

To begin this pedagogical re-visioning we will need much research into the ways students and teachers experience schooling in multiethnic contexts. As I have mentioned, research has in many ways stayed separated and segregated by race and language. Although skilled researchers must continue to investigate the linguistic and cultural negotiations of particular ethnic and linguistic in-groups, we also need work that seeks understanding across groups in addition to within them. My work is a small beginning in this direction. The limitations of my work are certainly significant. South Vista is one school. The eight youth I focused on and their sixty peers are but one multiethnic youth community. I am but one researcher without full access to the languages and cultures of the young people I came to know so deeply. Yet there is almost no work on the perspectives of Latino/as and their non-Spanish-speaking peers about Spanish use in multiethnic schools, on the language experiences of Pacific Islander youth in US schools, on AAL crossing and sharing by Latino/a and Pacific Islander students, or on the various youth texts that express identity within and across difference in schools like South Vista. We must redouble our efforts to build our knowledge of the multiethnic and multilingual schools of today and tomorrow if we are to have any hope of realizing the potential they offer.

The implications of my work at South Vista for pedagogy and curriculum are also considerable, and I have outlined them in detail at the conclusions of sections and chapters throughout. Before briefly summarizing the most important implications, let me sketch out the undergirding theoretical foundation they rest on. Working from sociocultural conceptions of language and literacy learning (and all learning) as situated in the cultural experiences of students' lives,[3] education researchers and theorists have developed various approaches to critical multicultural curriculum and pedagogy and various theories and practices of culturally relevant pedagogy. This scholarship has pushed for the equitable inclusion of the practices and histories of marginalized groups as a means of increasing student engagement and achievement by using these practices and histories as critical resources for academic learning.[4]

The complex ways oral and written language reinforced and blurred traditional notions of difference at South Vista challenges both researchers and teachers to consider how the resources students bring into such contexts differ from those they bring to less multiethnic settings. Further, they offer guidance about how such resources might help us modify the types of multiculturalism and language and literacy learning we promote in classrooms. Below, I outline several interrelated implications for teaching and learning in multiethnic contexts, building, at base, from sociocultural and critical learning theory.

At a broad level, culturally responsive teaching and curriculum and multicultural curriculum must contend with the tension between the need to honor the practices and positions of particular ethnic groups and the fact that youth do not always live ethnic divisions in the ways society and education (and research) has drawn them. This means that a pedagogy of pluralism in schools like South Vista must respond to the everyday realities of youth which include pluralist tendencies we have mainly failed to capitalize on in the classroom. Our teaching and curriculum should build on both the ways youth cross into and share practices *and* how they seek sustenance from the particular practices of their ethnic communities. To be clear, teaching and curriculum in such contexts must continue to support positive ethnic identity for all students, but to ignore such major crossing and sharing is to miss a vital opportunity. As teachers and researchers we must ask ourselves, what does cultural competence look like in the multiethnic spaces of our classrooms and communities? What would it mean to truly organize the curriculum on the various marginalized discourse positions in such multiethnic classrooms? Only with such understandings can we meaningfully seek to honor and extend the cultural competence of our young people.

Specific to the frustrations, desire to learn, and efforts at crossing and sharing in Spanish by African American and Pacific Islander youth in my study, we must continue efforts to reform additional language education in Spanish. The Spanish-speaking Latino/a population across the United States is rapidly growing. The non-Spanish-speaking students in my study wanted and needed access to Spanish but, like most schools, South Vista's Spanish classes isolated African American and Pacific Islander students from their Spanish-speaking peers and provided only one Spanish-speaking teacher. The *funds of knowledge* (Moll, 1992) that Spanish-speaking students bring to school should be used as resources both for the Latino/a students themselves in their quest to extend that knowledge and for those peers who desire access to those very same funds. At an even broader level, we should seek avenues to use the cultural and linguistic funds of all students in multiethnic and multilingual classrooms to foster both in-group and out-group linguistic and cultural dexterity and plurality. We should seek to *share the funds of knowledge* rather than use them for the in-group alone.

Such sharing was already happening in AAL at South Vista. The tremendous level of crossing and sharing in oral and written AAL and other cultural activities originating in Black culture suggests that teacher knowledge of the educational applications of AAL is needed even in communities where African Americans are not the majority. Furthermore, school is in an excellent position to be the site of critical language learning that could bolster the pride of African American youth about their linguistic heritage while simultaneously fostering more conscious respect from youth of other backgrounds about the language many of them use every day. This is particularly needed given the fact that African American youth are increasingly sharing communities, schools, and cultural and linguistic practices with young people of other backgrounds.

My work also has specific implications for our conceptions of literacy in multiethnic high schools. In particular, the ways *identity texts* resisted DAE writing conventions has important applications for English classrooms and other classrooms where writing happens. Teachers who assign and assess writing in multiethnic urban schools must recognize that the hyper-efficiency and AAL grammar and lexicon in youth texts are often not errors. Such texts present excellent resources for contrastive lessons about audience and purpose in writing. Youth texts at South Vista also pushed "writing" into complex multimodal territory. The blending of printed words with other symbols, with color, with sounds, and with performance suggests new forms of writing that classrooms must find ways to include and extend. Finally, the youth texts at South Vista indexed linguistic and ethnic identity in both form and content, revealing much about the genres and topics that should be included in the writing curriculum in multiethnic high schools.

I am calling for embracing a pedagogy of pluralism – a re-visioning of language, literacy, and humanities education in multiethnic contexts. Two major levers of this change are teacher knowledge and curriculum development. Teacher knowledge about the continuum of multiethnic youth space and about the linguistic and textual navigations in such spaces should be a top priority for teacher education and professional development. To achieve this increased knowledge about oral and written language in multiethnic schools, pre-service and practicing teachers must not only take courses on language, literacy, and difference, they must also engage in critical ethnographic and sociolinguistic inquiry with the young people in their classrooms. This has long been a call in the critical teacher education literature and this call has recently been renewed in light of changing demographics and increased knowledge about multiethnic schools.[5] Teacher educators must accept the challenge of preparing practitioners to enter their classrooms open to exploring language, ethnicity, and difference in the ways youth live them in multiethnic contexts. Teachers need to be prepared to recognize, embrace, and extend the dexterity and plurality of their students.

In addition to increased teacher knowledge toward more *multiculturally relevant* instruction, teachers and curriculum professionals charged with designing language, literacy, and humanities curricula must also attend to our emerging knowledge about multiethnic schools and communities. This will mean learning how to develop critical language and literacy curricula for specific multiethnic contexts by fusing teaching and learning theory, curriculum design techniques, and language and literacy research.[6]

The implications of my work for teaching and learning in multiethnic schools are set against the backdrop of our continued failure of vast numbers of urban youth. Disengagement, dropout, academic failure, and incarceration are common for our youth of color. All the while, youth of color *are* engaging in extraordinary linguistic and cultural practices that hold keys to our conceptions of learning and living together. We must join these resources with classroom learning. Table 7 lists these major implications.

The students in South Vista offered a window into understanding a grand American question: *how do we live together in a pluralistic society?* I spent a year trying to understand possible answers to this question in the cultural and linguistic lives of young people in multiethnic youth space. The answer, like identities and cultural practices, was not stable or singular. It pointed toward the possibilities of pluralistic sharing, and the necessities of in-group solidarity in the face of marginalizations of many kinds. It pointed to youths' continual struggle for voice and power in the face of dominant norms and expectations; to the small resistances enacted across the moments of their school days. It also, I hope, has begun to show how

Table 7. *Implications for teaching and learning in multiethnic schools*

Culturally relevant pedagogy & multicultural curriculum
Culturally relevant pedagogy and multicultural curriculum must
incorporate the ways youth live difference and division
Funds of knowledge
We should look to *share the funds of knowledge* rather than use them
for the educational benefit of the in-group alone
AAL teacher knowledge
Teachers may need knowledge about the educational applications of
AAL even if African American students are not the majority
Writing pedagogy
Youth texts incorporate multimedia and multiple modes that writing
pedagogy must learn to utilize
Teacher education
We must prepare teachers to recognize and utilize the ways oral and
written language reinforces ethnic division and creates conditions for
interethnic unity

understanding such multiethnic youth spaces can offer insights into
the practices youth cherish together and apart, and how school can
learn to cherish them too.

ROCHELLE AND THE SUNFLOWERS AGAIN

It is July 26th, 2007. School has been out over a month now. A summer
heatwave settles over the streets and homes of South Vista, a stifling
heat stretching out across the miles of the greater Metro area. I have
been reading Mike Rose's (1989) *Lives on the Boundary* again with
the pre-service teachers in my summer teacher education course and
I have been pondering some powerful words in his final chapter. We
need "a philosophy of language and literacy that affirms the diverse
sources of linguistic competence and deepens our understanding of
the ways class and culture blind us to the richness of those sources,"

(p. 238) writes Rose. And I've been thinking about how my work in the youth space of South Vista has been so much about revealing and understanding that richness in our increasingly multiethnic and multilingual schools – about what such sources have to offer our vision of language, literacy, difference, and schooling.

I am visiting Rochelle again today, checking in on her and her sunflowers nearly a month after we planted them amidst the many pots of her mother's flower garden. We've had a series of text messages about how tall the sunflowers are but, more importantly, I miss Rochelle and want to see how life is for her. I am bringing her mother a brilliant red hibiscus. It sits in full bloom in the passenger seat beside me.

It has been a couple of weeks since I have been in the community and it is nice to be driving in South Vista again. As I pull up to the house I see the potted flower garden again, lining the concrete walkway toward the house. The plants are not doing too well, not many blooms on the roses or lilies. They are cared for as before – well watered and trimmed. I can tell they are root-bound though, still waiting for space to flourish. Behind the many pots sits the bigger pot with the two sunflowers. They have grown a lot, thanks to Rochelle's watering. The sunflowers, too, are constrained by space. The smaller one is some three feet tall, the larger about four feet tall. Given the right environment they could easily grow twice that size. The larger plant is about to bloom, its ruby and gold flower held tight in a fist, just a day or two from bursting forth with color.

Inside the house we sit reminiscing about school and catching up. We talk a bit about her drama with Sharon, who has accused Rochelle of getting with her boyfriend, something Rochelle flatly denies. Rochelle tells me about her older brother who just moved back in last night. I hear him listening to music off in the garage. Later, he comes into the kitchen, looks at me and asks, "Who is you?" I tell him I am a friend of Rochelle's and that I am working with her at the school. His question reminds me how I have become so close to the youth in my work, but also about the intense ways I remain an outsider after all these months. Rochelle tells me they have thirty days to move. Rochelle considers the options, not sure whether the family will stay in South Vista, or move to some other neighboring city.

While we talk, the Maury Povich show provides more background sound. On the show, Povich is busy setting up pain; a young Black woman with two young Black men who claim to be the father of her child. The DNA test will show. Rochelle comments on how stupid people are for going on TV with their personal business. I agree. We stop talking and look at the show. I think of my love for my own father and how he was often absent during my childhood. And I think of the father Rochelle never speaks of.

Rochelle pulls us out of our private thoughts and, mercifully, away from the perpetuation of pain coming from the television. She asks me if I can take her to trade in her Jordan knock-offs at a local South Vista clothing shop. I agree and we hop in my old Volvo. A current hit by R&B artist Akon comes on and we talk about my custom speakers and how her brother's are the same only much larger. I skip to another song, a reggae affair from a mix CD I gave several youth in my study a couple of months before in return for some mixes they had given me. Rochelle laughs at me and shakes her head, "You is Jamaica, Django!" I laugh, too.

A cop car pulls behind us. It is one of the new souped-up Ram Chargers the city has recently purchased. I have heard many of the youth I know talk about being afraid of these powerful new cars and of the police. "I always think they after me when they get behind," Rochelle tells me. I agree and tell her I get nervous being followed. The cop turns onto another street. We let out a collective sigh and pull into the shop to trade in those Jordans.

When we get back to Rochelle's home I ask if I can take a picture of her and her sunflowers. I take one of Rochelle with the flowers and one of just the flowers. Figure 4 is the photo I took of the sunflowers that day. I will ask you to imagine the other photograph

Figure 4 Sunflowers go

to protect Rochelle's identity. In that photograph, Rochelle stands to the left of the sunflowers, in her pajama pants, wearing an old T-shirt with the words "You've already said too much!" emblazoned across the front. She is smiling broadly, the sun bright in her eyes, the sunflowers climbing up near shoulder height.

I say goodbye to Rochelle. It was great to see her and spend some more time with a person who has taught me so much. As I pull away from her house, my mind is swimming and trying to make meaning – temporary housing, Maury Povich reinforcing the pain of our fathers, police surveillance. The myriad issues pushing down on Rochelle and her family are so much bigger than school alone. And they are so much bigger than the scope of my work with Rochelle and the other youth I have come to know in South Vista. And yet all of their linguistic and cultural shouts of affirmation, all of their struggle for agency, for voice, and power is set against these bigger

Figure 5 Ma plants go

social problems which themselves are tied so deeply to dominant narratives of race and ethnicity, of class and language.

I think about school being one important lever that can help to dig us and our young people out of these narratives, out of the eternal *educational debt* (Ladson-Billings, 2006) and social debt owed to marginalized youth and communities for centuries of scholastic oppression and continuing disservice. I think about how many hours youth spend in school and about what those hours can do to change things.

As I leave Rochelle's house and head toward the freeway I think again as I often do even now of her multimedia text in June.

My plants are right with the world, they are in a state of flourishing with their environment; they *go*. And I ponder what it would take to make school *go* and what it would take to help Rochelle and her peers *go* in school. What it would take for school to hear and support their shouts of linguistic and cultural affirmation. What is "the richness of those sources" and how can school and youth come together to use those sources to learn how to flourish in a pluralistic world? How can school learn about oral and written language and difference to revise the old and broken visions of power and plurality?

On the freeway I speed along through the heatwave. I feel at the end of something, and at the beginning. I have learned so much from Rochelle, Carla, Rahul, Gloria, Miles, Julio, Ela, Carlos, and all of their peers. I have learned about how they stay together in difference and about how a caring and knowledgeable society could make these negotiations work to increase interethnic understanding, linguistic and cultural competence and pride, and engagement with school as a transformative space. I have learned about how we can help youth flourish in multiethnic urban communities, how we can give them the space to grow, release them from the monocultural programs binding them to assimilate or fail. How we can help young people learn as we learn from them about what it means to live within and across difference in a multiethnic and multilingual society.

How we can make school *go*, and *go*.

Appendix: Notes on methodology in cultural studies of language across difference

Investigating oral and written language as it challenged and reinforced ethnic difference did not fall neatly into any one methodological box. This is not a new problem in applied social language and educational research. The complex real-world problems of interest to applied social linguists and educational researchers rarely fit into the theory or methodology of any one discipline. My work with youth in South Vista attempted to bring together knowledge about oral and written language at various micro and macro levels as it mapped out experiences of difference, division, and unity and as it relates to educational theory and practice. Such social, cultural, and linguistic terrain demanded several methods of collection and analysis from the distinct, but complementary disciplines of sociolinguistics, linguistic anthropology, critical discourse analysis, language and literacy studies in education and, more generally, cultural anthropology.

Given the need to span techniques of collection and analysis, I brought together several methodologies. In order to understand the ways oral and written language reinforced and challenged lines of ethnic and linguistic difference at South Vista, I needed both data documenting linguistic, literate, and social interaction *and* data focused on how youth made sense of such culturally situated practices. I collected roughly four types of data: fieldnote (of interactions inside and outside the classroom), textual (e.g., rap lyrics and text messages), photographic (mainly of youth texts), and interview (both sociolinguistic and ethnographic).

In this appendix I will provide some discussion of my shifting roles and purposes throughout the fieldwork and the various approaches I employed in interpreting the cultural and linguistic data I gathered at South Vista. In order to explore this methodological terrain, I will focus on the various tools of data collection and the various lenses of data analysis I used to understand just one piece of data: Ela's backpack text that I analyzed in Chapter 5 (See Figure 1 and analysis pp. 129–131). This exploration of my methodological moves will serve as a window into how I borrowed from and merged various fields to come to an understanding of how oral and written language challenged and reinforced difference at South Vista.

SEEING THROUGH THE LENSES OF ETHNOGRAPHY
AND THE SOCIAL LANGUAGE FIELDS

My general methodological orientation in this book might be initially described as critical discourse analysis (CDA) in that I am interested in the analysis of relationships of power and privilege, equity and access as they are enacted through stretches of everyday oral and written language. In approaching such stretches of oral and written language I work from a modified version of Norman Fairclough's definition of discourse as language in social and cultural practice.[1] This definition moves beyond the basic disciplinary definition used in linguistics of discourse as language beyond the sentence level and foregrounds a commitment to understanding language as it is used and thought about by individuals and their communities. In addition, this definition allows for a simultaneous focus on micro linguistic features below the sentence level and macro linguistic content in larger stretches of language, so, for instance, both grammar and ethnic identity can be approached as discursive content and as units of analysis. Fairclough defines CDA as

> A theoretical perspective on language and more generally semiosis as one element of the material social process, which gives rise to ways of analysing language or semiosis within broader analyses of the social process ... It is a theory or method which is in dialogic relationship with other social theories and methods, which should engage in a 'transdisciplinary' rather than just an interdisciplinary way.
>
> (2001b, p. 121)

For me, this necessary transdisciplinarity in CDA represents a number of conceptual and methodological lenses through which to view any given piece of discourse. These lenses push beyond CDA as an initial description of my methodology to include knowledge, tools, and theoretical and epistemological commitments from other social language fields and from cultural anthropology. In what follows I seek to illuminate the ways each of these lenses helped me interpret Ela's backpack text as they helped me to interpret all of the oral and written language I analyze in this book. Figure 6 is the photograph I took of Ela's backpack text in the back of her biology class.

LENS ONE: DESCRIBING SOCIOLINGUISTIC FEATURES
AND ETHNIC IDENTITY CLAIMS

My preliminary lens focuses on describing the surface language of the text. I begin by leaning on knowledge developed by the quantitative sociolinguistic

Figure 6 True Hamoz gurl fo lyph

variationist paradigm.[2] This paradigm of understanding language variation and change by correlating social categories to linguistic variables through statistical analysis has become the dominant one in sociolinguistics. Although I myself engage in the qualitative social language work of discourse analysis, the ethnography of communication, and linguistic anthropology, the knowledge developed through quantitative sociolinguistics allows me a descriptive entry point to treat certain linguistic features as AAL. In looking at Ela's backpack text, for example, I notice an interesting feature of AAL phonology that has been represented by Ela in print. She has chosen to write "fo" rather than the DAE "for," an example of r-vocalization. Knowledge built by variationist scholars allows me to see this as a common feature in AAL and some US Southern and Northern Englishes, and to know it is marked as AAL in South Vista and in many US urban communities with large African American populations.

Also from a descriptive sociolinguistic perspective, I notice Ela's spellings of "Superwymen," "Gurl," "Lyph," and "wut" as examples of "eye dialect" (alternative spelling that does not change the sound, but indexes vernacular language). I can link up with later work in the variationist tradition on AAL and Hip Hop Nation Language (HHNL) to entertain the possibility that these spellings are conscious acts of linguistic identity.[3]

Still working from an understanding of Hip Hop language, though this one a localized understanding, I note the phrase "Wut it do do!!" as a greeting (translated in DAE as "What's going on?") associated with the local Hip Hop movement of South Vista and the surrounding metro area known as Hyphy. To give broader perspective to these textual representations of AAL and eye dialect, I compare Ela's text with other written representations of AAL from the multiethnic youth space of South Vista. This comparison shows Ela's African American, Latino/a, and Pacific Islander peers employing such AAL, HHNL, and eye dialect spellings in their text messages and rap lyrics, as well as in the writing on their objects and public spaces.

Through this preliminary descriptive lens of the surface language, I also might remark on Ela's use of the word "Hamoz" (Samoan) from a multilingualism perspective, thinking as well of language choice work stretching back to Fishman's (1965) seminal question "Who speaks what language to whom and where?", or more recent code-switching and language choice studies which posit lexical or phrase-level switches as rational choices based on communicative context.[4]

And, of course, in even a cursory surface-level description of Ela's backpack as a piece of discourse, I would note the reappropriation of the Superman symbol into the possibly feminist statement "Superwymen" and the bold ethnic identity claims "Samoan Pride" and "True Hamoz gurl fo lyph" (true Samoan girl for life).

Yet leaning on sociolinguistic and language choice perspectives and noting possible ethnic and gendered identity claims does little for understanding what these claims might mean to Ela and her Pacific Islander, Latino/a, and African American peers. Nor what Samoan or AAL or Hip Hop language might mean to Ela or whether she uses these languages in oral communication within and across ethnicity. While some discourse analysts might stop at this point and use their own schemes and those of the various disciplines to complete an interpretation, from a sociocultural perspective interested in the meanings participants attach to uses of oral and written language in multiethnic settings, I need understanding which reaches beyond the piece of oral or written language itself. And I need to understand how a search for power and voice is operating in the linguistic and literate choices Ela has written across her backpack and how these choices relate to my organizing questions of challenging and reinforcing notions of difference and division.

LENS TWO: PARTICIPANT OBSERVATION IN ACTIVITIES OF MUTUAL CONCERN

Working from traditions of ethnography and qualitative methodology[5] and linguistic anthropology,[6] I can achieve a deeper and more critical analysis of language, identity, and ethnicity in Ela's backpack text from the activity of prolonged participant observation in her linguistic world. Participant observation has long been deemed the hallmark method of ethnographic and linguistic anthropological fieldwork. It is seen as a necessary research activity for describing and explaining the relationships between language, culture, and society.

Learning about cultural and linguistic worlds from participants through participant observation means being a participant observer at times, an observer at other times, and a participant at still other times. That is, although we often pass all ethnographic work off as "participant observation," the fact is that such a research activity falls along a continuum. When I was sitting in the back of classrooms jotting down fieldnotes I was primarily an observer, whereas when I was playing basketball at the community or school gym I was primarily a participant. In each of these circumstances I was gathering understanding, but my role as a member of the activities shifted throughout my research. Yet humanization between researchers and participants is not achieved through taking fieldnotes in the back of classrooms or on park benches. Genuine relationships and moments of cultural understanding are fostered in authentic participation in activities that matter to the participants.

A second methodological lens necessary to understand Ela's sense of Samoaness and her connection to and use of the Samoan language, then, is through participating in activities and cultural spaces where these facets of ethnic and linguistic identity are used. One activity that I participated in throughout the year was basketball. Basketball is a love of my life beyond research and it was a love of many of the youth I worked with as well. The vignette describing my Samoan language lesson during basketball practice (see Chapter 3, pp. 56–59) is an example of such authentic participation in basketball which resulted in ever-deeper understandings of the role of the Samoan language in Ela's sense of ethnic and linguistic self.

It was through basketball as well as our shared island heritage that Ela and I formed our early relationship. This relationship and the conversations and activities it centered on allowed us both to think about the place of Samoa and Jamaica in our current lives and about what basketball did to bring us together with peers across ethnicity. On that day I took the impromptu Samoan lesson on the side of the basketball court, it was the authenticity of place and activity and relationship that allowed me a small glimpse into a language that had few spaces for voice in school and the community. Later, when Ela invited my wife and me to the Samoan church where Ela used the Samoan language in song and service and conversation, I would have further occasions to understand Ela's sense of Samoaness and connection to the Samoan language. But it was the confluence of basketball, language, and our ethnic identities I describe in the vignette that created the public space in school for Ela to begin sharing her linguistic knowledge and identity.

After considering the ethnographic and sociolinguistic event of authentic participant observation embedded in basketball practice, the significance of Ela's use of "Hamoz" on her backpack texts is put into stark relief. Further understandings I gathered through participant observation about how hyper-marginalized Samoan was in the face of Spanish, spoken as at least one of the languages of 70 percent of students, and AAL, used as the lingua franca in multiethnic youth space, gives me an even deeper analytic sense of what one Samoan word embedded in her backpack text might mean in Ela's negotiation of language and identity and power in her youth community. This second lens of participant observation in activities of mutual concern, then, allows me to begin an interpretation of the sociolinguistic features of Ela's texts from a more emic perspective – one that is necessary in any cultural analysis of language.

LENS THREE: THE ETHNOGRAPHIC INTERVIEW

To further engage in a critical social language analysis which attempts to understand the relationship between social and cultural power and meaning in language use, I also need to know Ela's sense-making about her text to layer upon my initial descriptive work and her participation in linguistic and cultural activities inside and outside the classroom. Along with participant observation, ethnographic interviews have long been the key data-gathering tool of cultural anthropology. Such ethnographic interviews can be used to gain insider perspective on the purpose of language use and language choices. These insider perspectives allow me to link up with *speech act* theory and the ethnography of communication forwarded by Hymes (1972) as an alternative trajectory to quantitative sociolinguistics. Seeing Ela's text as a speech act means I am interested in her understandings of the norms and expectations of putting texts on self and object as they are situated in her multiethnic and multilingual speech community.

The interview excerpt I shared and analyzed in Chapter 5 (pp. 132–134) is an example of Ela's sense-making about the ways she communicates linguistic and ethnic identity through youth space written language. You will remember that in the interview Ela shared the notebooks she kept in her backpack where she inscribed messages of Samoaness using English and Samoan language, flowers, and bamboo-style lettering. She also told me in the interview of her plans to get these messages permanently tattooed on her skin.

These layers of ethnographic content shared in the context of an interview further assist me in a critical social language analysis of Ela's backpack text. For one thing, the bamboo-style lettering in "Samoan Pride" becomes important. Even more important are Ela's plans to make a permanent public commitment to ethnic and linguistic identity claims by inking the message on her legs. And the intensity of her Samoaness as she navigates her multiethnic and multilingual youth space is clear in the messages of love and commitment (e.g., Ela's notebook message, "Alofa Samoa" (Love Samoa)). This interview and other interviews let me see Ela's uses of oral and written Samoan and ethnic identity claims in youth space and other spaces through the lens of her attitudes and knowledge in addition to my own as analyst.

LENS FOUR: THE ETHNOLINGUISTIC INTERVIEW
AND FIELDNOTES

To further deepen my critical social language analysis of Ela's backpack text, I also want to look at her use of AAL in oral communication to shed light on the depth of her linguistic relationship to AAL and to put her use of r-vocalization ("fo" for "for") in the context of Ela as a language user. One source of data about Ela as an AAL user is my interviews with her over the year.

Although all my interviews were ethnographic interviews with certain content objectives, at times I was less concerned with ethnographic content and more concerned with linguistic content. Linking up again with the sociolinguistic variationist tradition, I borrow the tool of the sociolinguistic interview. In the sociolinguistic interview, the interviewer attempts to elicit vernacular talk from the participant to gather examples of variables of interest (the "danger of death" question being the famous example – where the interviewer asks the interviewee to describe a time her/his life was in danger).[7] Sometimes, of course, it was in these less structured moments of the interview that some of the most telling cultural content emerged and it is folly to imagine a clean split between a sociolinguistic interview and an ethnographic one.[8] However, I was conscious to pay attention to both the need for youth sense-making and the need for some everyday talk to get at my interests in language and difference within and across ethnicity. I came to see this dual-purpose interview as an *ethnolinguistic interview* and I hope you see evidence of both the cultural and the linguistic in my analysis of the interview data in this book. I also hope this dual-purpose interview can be nuanced and extended by other researchers interested in both the cultural and the linguistic.[9]

My ethnolinguistic interviews with Ela allowed her to display the full range of AAL grammar (see Table 4, p. 89), lexicon, and phonology. As I have shown throughout the book, ethnographic and social language fieldnotes were also a key tool I used to record uses of language in interaction between youth at South Vista.[10] In the hundreds of pages of fieldnotes I recorded at South Vista High and in the broader city of South Vista, I noted Ela using every major grammatical feature of AAL (from the habitual be to zero copula). In addition, I noted her use of AAL and HHNL lexical items (e.g., "ashy," "nigga," "Hyphy") and her participation in signifying and ritual insult (again see Chapter 4 for examples).

This deep linguistic participation in AAL and Hip Hop language allows me to see Ela's use of AAL, HHNL, and eye dialect on her backpack and in her other youth space writing as connected to her linguistic and youth cultural identity. I can interpret it, then, in the context of Ela as a language user rather than simply from my own sociolinguistic knowledge of AAL and youth language, or worse, rather than simply interpreting it as an error or an anomaly in her written language.

Coupled with youth sense-making across ethnic groups about the pervasiveness of AAL sharing and socialization and the limited use of Pacific Islander languages in school and community, Ela's uses of these languages in interviews and interaction lets me situate her backpack text culturally and linguistically into my interpretive scheme of challenging and reinforcing difference and division in multiethnic youth space.

INTERPRETING THROUGH MULTIPLE LENSES

I have attempted to show you the methodological lenses through which I practice gathering and interpreting oral and written language as a window into how youth of color are challenging and reinforcing ethnic and linguistic difference in changing multiethnic communities. Ela's text, of course, is but one small instance of language in social and cultural practice in the multiethnic and multilingual youth space of South Vista. However, working through the multiple sources of data necessary for a culturally situated interpretation of the writing Ela inscribed on her backpack can help illuminate what I actually do over months of fieldwork and analysis rather than the all-too-common discussion of methods in the abstract.[11]

Even with these multiple lenses through which to understand the oral and written language of Ela and her peers, my interpretations are only a glimpse into how youth live difference through language in contemporary urban contexts. This will always be true in cultural linguistic analysis. And yet each methodological layer, each set of tools and theoretical commitments, offers an ever fuller interpretation – one closer to the way Ela, her peers, and her community navigate language and self in the face of demographic change and continued inequities.

Knowledge built in the quantitative sociolinguistic paradigm layers upon participation in activities of mutual concern. I better understand the meaning of language and identity in these activities through ethnographic interviews where youth share perspectives and possibilities. At their most informal moments, these interviews also offer glimpses into language use which layer again upon the linguistic features, the cultural activities, and the youth sense-making. There is the photograph, too, which gives me a still target to consider through these lenses over many, many months. These layers, these lenses, are not linear, of course, but are iterative and recursive at once – representing the methodological weaving together of meaning over time.

And always there are relationships of dignity and care with participants which, as I described in the introductory chapter, are necessary to glimpse insider truths and, more important, to avoid colonization by working toward humanization for both the researcher and the participants.

TOWARD HUMANIZING INQUIRY

I did not go far enough in my work with Ela and her peers. My relationships with them over the year were strong and each of them told me explicitly that they learned much from our time together, that they enjoyed the process of research with me. And I remain connected to many of their lives; attending their high-school graduations years after the study, writing letters of recommendation for jobs or college, texting about relationships or fights or college admission, checking-in when crisis or transition happens: for humanizing research does not end when the study does. But I continually question whether it was worth it for them, whether those months of humanization between us influenced their lives in important enough ways.

I also must remind myself that ending the colonizing inquiry of looking for deficits in the cultures of oppressed communities, of treating participants like subjects, of pretending our relationships with them did not change us, of seeking to take but not to give, that ending colonizing inquiry is a movement and I am one small member. Many in the research community have done a far better job than I and I will continue to grow as a humanizing researcher. For many researchers, relationships of care and dignity and dialogic consciousness-raising during the research make far greater an impact on participants and on the community than I made. For now I must reckon with how I can continue to humanize the cultural communities of my work as I myself was humanized by the young people in those communities.

One important step in this direction is in the way I have represented myself and the youth in this book. Others will judge whether this book represents the youth and their worlds with the care and dignity I experienced as I conducted fieldwork. And others will judge whether the knowledge I share in this book is helpful in extending our understanding of pluralist societies and in improving teaching and learning in schools serving multiethnic communities. But I have worked to represent Ela and her peers with dignity as I argue for change and understanding as a result of what I learned from them.

In June, 2009, two years after my fieldwork at South Vista, I went to see Rahul and Ela and Rochelle graduate from high school. It had been more than a year since I saw them and there were many embraces and handshakes to go around. I took photos with Ela and Rochelle and many other youth I came to know at South Vista. I also took a photo with Rahul after the ceremony. In the photo we are both staring ahead smiling, proud of his accomplishment and, I think, proud of being there for each other. As I finish writing this book, there are great distances between me and Rahul. I sit at my desk looking at that photo of us at his graduation. As I consider the photo, four lines from Rahul's rap I shared in Chapter 1 echo through my head:

> HE IS A FRIEND WHO UNDERTSTAND FULLY
> HE KNOWS WAT WE GO THROUGH
> CAUSE HE'S BEEN THROUH IT
> HE'S INSPIRED ME THE WAY AND TOLD ME TO DO IT, TO IT

We can be friends with our participants. We can, in small ways, come to understand. We can inspire them as they inspire us. We can humanize through the act of research.

Notes

I BEGINNINGS: SHOUTS OF AFFIRMATION FROM
   SOUTH VISTA

1 I use pseudonyms for people and places throughout this book to preserve anonymity.

2 None of the participants in my previous teaching and research at South Vista High remained at the school during the current study.

3 The White population of the city is small and is mainly geographically separated by a major freeway which cuts across the city limits.

4 See Klein (2004) and Smelser *et al.* (2001) for national and urban US population trends.

5 See Eisenhart and Howe (1992) for an early review and discussion of alternative conceptions of validity in interpretive research.

6 I have preserved all youth spelling and grammar of the texts I analyze throughout the book.

7 AAL is also called African American Vernacular English, African American English, and Ebonics. I follow Smitherman (2006) and others in using AAL because the term foregrounds the importance, linguistic distinctiveness, and alternative cultural history of AAL in relation to other Englishes.

8 See Alim (2006) for a thorough discussion of HHNL and Alim, Ibrahim, and Pennycook (2009) for research on the global reach of HHNL.

9 As Geertz (1973) told us long ago, "Cultural analysis is intrinsically incomplete" (p. 29).

10 See Briggs (1986), Emerson, Fretz, and Shaw (1995), and Geertz (1973) for discussion and evidence on the goals of insider understanding.

11 See Peshkin (1993), Guba and Lincoln (2005), Charmaz (2005), and Howe (2009) for discussion dedicated to the positivist influences and ongoing tensions on questions of rigor, validity, and truth in qualitative inquiry.

12 This general belief is becoming widespread in the literature on critical ethnography, critical qualitative research, and critical social language research in communities of color and other marginalized and oppressed communities. See Guba and Lincoln (2005) for a discussion of the connections between

validity, social impact, and relationship building, Zentella (1997) for a discussion of *anthropolitical linguistics* as social language work that honors survival and pushes for social change, and Morrell (2004) and Irizarry (2011) for examples of urban youth of color participating in the research process as a means to critical consciousness.

13 See Bucholtz and Hall (2004), Gee (2001), Hall, Hubert, and Thompson (1996), and Rampton (2006) for scholarship conceptualizing identity and language in late modernity.

14 See Alim (2004), Baugh (1999), and Morgan (2002) for such studies focused on African Americans, and Cintron (1997), Guerra (1998), Valdés (1996), and Zentella (1997) for studies focused on Latino/as.

15 See Ball (2006), Ladson-Billings (2006), and Kozol (2005) for discussions of contemporary US school segregation, Massey (2001) for research on contemporary urban segregation of communities of color, and Klein (2004) and Smelser *et al.* (2001) for national and urban population trends.

16 See Heath (1983), Labov (1972), and Smitherman (1977) for early sociolinguistic research illustrating the ways the linguistic resources of African Americans (and, for Heath, poor Southern European Americans as well) can be used in classroom pedagogy and testing. See Moll (1992) for such research in bilingual Mexican American communities and Garcia (1993) for an excellent early review of research on cultural and linguistic practices as educational resources across communities of color in the US.

17 See Ball (1999), Paris and Ball (2009), and Valdés (1996) for a complete review of this movement over time in US schooling and research.

18 Gutiérrez and Rogoff (2003) use the term *repertoires of practice* to conceptualize the variation and diversity of linguistic and cultural practices of individuals and communities, advocating that schools should foster and extend such repertoires.

19 Harris (2006) and Rampton (2006) are examples of this tradition in British Cultural Studies.

20 In another important study, Harris (2006) has followed this work and, like Rampton, taken ethnographic and sociolinguistic methodologies into multiethnic youth communities in British urban high-school settings.

21 See Jørgensen (2008) for a discussion of his concepts of *polylingualism* and *languaging* developed from his and others' research with urban youth in late modern Europe. Polylingualism – akin to my terms *linguistic dexterity* and *linguistic plurality* – describes late modern urban contexts in which youth use any and all linguistic resources at their disposal even if they are not completely fluent or multilingual in all given languages in a social context.

Languaging – akin to my term *language sharing* – describes the act of sharing in features of multiple languages in multilingual contexts.

22 See Eckert (1989) for a discussion of local prestige and language variation.

23 See Fought (2006) and Harris (2006) for further empirical discussions of the relationship between language and ethnic identity.

24 Le Page and Tabouret-Keller (1985) coined the conception of language as an *act of identity* in their work in multilingual Belize.

25 This is the type of *strategic agency* Spivak (1989, and in Landry and MacLean, 1996) speaks of as possibly available to the oppressed in the face of social orders constraining larger acts of power.

26 I find Bakhtin's (1981) metaphor of the centrifuge particularly helpful in analyzing the forces influencing the practices of multiethnic youth space. Bakhtin called the centralizing forces pulling social actors toward dominant language use *centripetal forces* and the decentralizing forces pulling social actors toward marginalized language use *centrifugal forces*. At South Vista I will show that these forces were enacted through complex relationships between individuals (e.g., grandparents, teachers, peers), cultural communities (e.g., African Americans, Hip Hoppers), ideologies (about the worth of certain languages and literacies and certain groups of people), and institutions (e.g., schools).

27 This is what Burke (1969) theorized as *division* in social interaction and *identification* in social interaction. For Burke, a central organizing force in human interaction is that we work to identify *with* others to persuade them of our goals and come to agreement and we work to divide ourselves *from* others if we believe they are so unlike us in our given goals that they cannot be persuaded of our goals.

28 This is, indeed, the major project of scholarship about and by people of color across the twentieth century of the social sciences.

29 Hindi is listed here with Pacific Islander languages as all Hindi speakers at the school were Fijian Indian with parents of East Indian descent who were born and raised in Fiji.

30 The ø symbol is used to mark the AAL optional omission of the copular verb "is" or "are." This and other AAL features in this interaction are discussed further in Chapter 4.

31 I use italics throughout data examples to mark the features of language, youth and Hip Hop lexicon, and ethnic or local urban affiliations in speech that are the subject of my analysis.

32 "Y'all" is also a common feature in Southern American White speech, but is highly marked as Black in this West Coast city.

33 I use "Dominant American English" instead of the commonly used "Standard English" to foreground unequal power relationships between the dominant American English and other American Englishes.

34 See Green (2002) for a full discussion of AAL verbal paradigms.

35 "ing" to "in" (ŋ→n) is also a common consonant replacement in other non-dominant Englishes throughout the world.

36 See Green (2002) for a full discussion of speech events in African American Language.

2   "SPANISH IS BECOMING FAMOUS": YOUTH PERSPECTIVES
      ON SPANISH IN A CHANGING YOUTH COMMUNITY

1 Although my comprehension of Spanish is decent from two years living and teaching middle school ESL in the Dominican Republic, my production has never been particularly strong. My comprehension ability allowed me to understand much of the interactions between youth in Spanish, though I make no attempt to do the type of detailed linguistic analysis of these interactions that I do of AAL interactions in Chapter 4. In addition, my interviews and interactions with Latino/a youth were conducted almost entirely in English, with occasional lexical or phrase-level switches from either the youth or me. This is not a major limitation in interview content as each of these youth was a relatively balanced bilingual, fluent in English, and had 10–15 years living and attending school in the United States. It does mean, though, that the approximations of the vernacular I recorded in sociolinguistic interviews were the Englishes of these Latino/a youth, not the various Spanishes they also used. Even given this limitation, the perspectives about Spanish use and the interactions with Spanish language I analyze in this chapter provide vital knowledge about the severely understudied topic of the role of Spanish in changing multiethnic schools and communities in the United States.

2 See Valdés and Figueroa (1994) for an in-depth discussion of the complex issues involved in measuring bilingualism.

3 Again see Valdés and Figueroa (1994) for this term and further terms for classifying bilinguals based on life experience and proficiency.

4 A model of this type of conscious or rational code-switching is detailed in Myers-Scotton and Bolonyai (2001) from their work in multilingual Kenya.

5 Carlos was struggling to articulate a theory of language choice. Although he was conscious of macro factors, like the ethnicity of the interlocutor, other important factors are below the level of consciousness. Fishman (1965) outlines the major factors involved in language choice as group membership, situation or setting, and topic.

6 Both of these local notions did have elements of sociolinguistic truth. AAL, spoken by all the Black youth in my study, does have important grammatical relations to West African languages and to English-based creoles that emerged from the trade of African slaves (Baugh, 1999; Rickford and Rickford, 2000) I will explore AAL in depth in Chapter 4.

7 The role of adult family and community use in language shift and maintenance has been shown to be the crucial factor in addition to the role of school (Fishman, 1991).

8 Bakhtin's (1981) metaphor of the centrifuge is helpful here in thinking about the forces at play in Carla's Spanish language use and proficiency. For Carla and other Latino/a youth, the pull of elders and peers were certainly *centrifugal forces* pulling them against the dominant stream of Englishes demanded in school, youth space, and the broader society.

9 This pride in Spanish is somewhat at odds with findings in Olsen's (1997) study of immigrant high-school students where she found shame in Spanish use. One explanation for this is that the proportion of Latino/as was far higher in South Vista than in the school in Olsen's study.

10 Zentella's (1997) study of a Puerto Rican neighborhood in New York City revealed a similar pipeline of Spanish speakers that replaced speakers who had shifted toward English dominance.

11 See Lippi-Green (1997) for research into such discriminatory language ideologies, particularly as they are enacted around the accents of native Spanish speakers in the US.

12 Outside of school, most youth across groups, regardless of gender, maintained friendships within their ethnic group. All eight of the focus students in my work spent most or all of their peer time outside school with friends of their own ethnic background. At school, however, this gender/ethnic relationship difference was fairly pronounced.

13 Such *he-said-she-said* speech acts among girls and African American girls in particular have been the subject of important work in linguistic anthropology (Goodwin, 1980, 1990).

14 Although the complex tense/aspect system, lexicon, and the semantics of certain speech events of AAL can exclude a DAE speaker from comprehending meaning, I will show in Chapter 4 that many Latino/a and Pacific Islander youth understood and participated in these features.

15 See Hill (2001) for research on what she terms the *mock Spanish* use of White speakers in casual interactions and popular media. Hill argues persuasively that these uses reinforce dominant language ideologies which hold Spanish as inferior.

16 See Goodwin (2002) for a review of this literature which has not yet dealt ably with cross-ethnic linguistic and social relationships.

17 I follow Gal (1991) here in searching for interpretations that reposition dominant Western narratives of gender roles, which have positioned females as passive and silent.

18 Again see Hill (2001).

19 See Hymes (1972) for the original formulation of *speech act* theory.

20 I explore ritual insult across ethnicity at South Vista in Chapter 4.

21 See Moje *et al.* (2004), Moll (1992), Moll and Gonzales (1994) for examples of using the funds of knowledge of Latino/a students in formal classroom learning.

3   "TRUE SAMOAN": ETHNIC SOLIDARITY AND
    LINGUISTIC REALITY

1 I participated 2–3 times weekly as a player, not a coach.

2 I group Hindi here with Pacific Islander languages as it was the primary home language of Rahul and the other Fijian Indian youth at the school.

3 Work in educational anthropology on other newer immigrant urban populations, like Southeast Asian communities, has only just begun (Lee, 2002; Stritikus and Nguyen, 2007), though this work is not linguistically focused.

4 This finding builds importantly on Wei, Milroy, and Ching's (2001) work on the role of the Chinese Christian church in language maintenance among Chinese bilinguals living in Britain, especially for the younger generations.

5 Tongan and Fijian youth also attended Christian churches with their respective ethnic communities.

6 This was all embedded, of course, in the painful history of colonization and its relationship with Christianity, though my analysis here remains focused on the facets of linguistic and ethnic identity youth participated in at church.

7 Although not a linguistic assessment, I observed Ela's fluency and literacy at her home, her church, and in our interviews.

8 There are important similarities here to the sorts of linguistic shame and language choices Bonner (2004) documented among Garifuna youth in Belize, who were small in number and where Belize Creole had eclipsed their heritage language in the broader youth culture.

9 There are interesting implications in Ela's statement for theories of language and identity. Le Page and Tabouret-Keller's (1985) model of language as an *act of identity* focuses on behaviors and an individual's ability to take on an identity and become a member based on those behaviors. This is true of Gee's (1999) work on *Discourses* as well. But as Ela reports, language is one

primary factor in being accepted, but also works in concert with group members ratifying a speaker as a member based on other attributes, like phenotype, as well.

10 Ela used the AAL grammatical feature, the *habitual be* in "She *be talking* Samoan to me." The *habitual be* is part of the complex tense and aspect system of AAL that I discuss in depth in Chapter 4.

11 Bakhtin's (1981) notion of *centripetal forces* is again useful here as a theoretical lens through which to view the centralizing forces of school and youth culture pulling Ela and her Pacific Islander peers toward the use of Englishes even as the decentralizing forces of home, elders, church, and future plans pulled them (with less force) toward heritage language use.

12 See Gifford and Valdés (2006) for an excellent discussion of current debates in bilingual education in the US for Latino/as which increasingly include "English Only" policies that isolate Spanish speakers from instruction in their heritage language. See also Romaine (1995) for macro-level analysis of bilingual education in global perspective and discussions of the role of discriminatory language ideologies playing out in the lack of policy and educational commitments to certain languages (like Spanish in US contexts).

13 See Bonner (2004) for a thorough discussion of local language loss, Crystal (2000) for a global perspective on language death, and Fishman (1991) for a statement of the factors involved in language shift.

14 See Dewey (1938) and Freire (1970) for the theoretical foundation of *problem posing* education. I discuss the theoretical foundations further in the Interlude following Chapter 4.

15 In his study of language and literacy in a Mexicano community in the Midwestern United States, Guerra (1998) terms these spaces of cultural and linguistic safety for marginalized groups *home fronts*, denoting their connection to national, neighborhood, and heritage languages.

4   "THEY'RE IN MY CULTURE, THEY SPEAK THE SAME
     WAY": SHARING AFRICAN AMERICAN LANGUAGE AT
     SOUTH VISTA

1 Some seminal examples from these decades of AAL scholarship: Baugh (1983), Labov (1972), Rickford and Rickford (2000), and Smitherman (1977, 2006).

2 Of course, not all African Americans speak AAL. Like any language variety, it is socially and culturally learned and used. Only people who learn it and have reason to use it do so. Although this learning is often tied to race for reasons of segregation and solidarity, it is not always tied to race as evidenced by the youth of South Vista.

3 I use the N-words (plural) in keeping with Smitherman (2006), who has found at least eight meanings of the words in her study of AAL semantics and lexicon.

4 See Green (2002) and Rickford and Rickford (2000) for a complete sociolinguistic discussion of all grammatical and phonological rules in this chapter, unless otherwise noted.

5 I use the term *ethnolinguistic* to describe interviews with both the ethnographic aims of gathering insider perspectives and the sociolinguistic aims of collecting everyday language use (see Appendix for a thorough discussion of my methodology).

6 See Smitherman (2006) for a current list of AAL terms and sayings.

7 See Smitherman (2006) for the most current essay on signifying and the dozens.

8 See Carpio (2008) and Rickford and Rickford (2000).

9 See Smitherman (2006) for a thorough treatment of the term in Black and Hip Hop culture.

10 I should note that the AAL lexicon and Hip Hop lexicon have a close relationship, with many Hip Hop terms finding a place in the vocabulary of AAL speakers, just as many AAL terms have always been a part of Hip Hop culture. Alim (2006) calls the relationship between the AAL lexicon and the Hip Hop nation lexicon a "familial one," denoting this strong dialogic relationship.

11 Sierra also participated here in the phonological feature, the consonant replacement "ing" to "in" ($\eta \rightarrow n$). This is a feature common to AAL and other non-dominant Englishes, but was marked as AAL at South Vista.

12 Although there was considerable variation in how much AAL youth used in interviews, my purpose here is simply to provide evidence that they did, in fact, use features of AAL in interviews. AAL features in these interviews also show the persistence of AAL use beyond everyday youth interactions as I was the primary interlocutor. I omit Gloria from this table as she rarely used features of AAL grammar in interviews, though she did participate in the AAL lexicon. Gloria did not have any strong relationships with African American youth at school or in the community, which explains why her use of AAL was less pronounced than the other focus youth in my work.

13 All of the Mexican/Mexican American students I interviewed often used multiple negation structures. I do not represent them here as such constructions are also a feature of Chicano English (Fought, 2006). Other features used by Latino/a youth in interviews, like the habitual be and zero copula, are not features of Chicano English. In addition, it is important to point out that features like multiple negation are common in other non-dominant Englishes in the United States and globally, though the features I analyze in this book were marked as AAL in this West Coast US city.

14 See Rickford and Rickford (2000) for further elaboration on the *existential it's*.

15 It is important to note that Collins (2004) argues that the media's objectification of Jennifer Lopez should be seen in the context of Black women's subjection in the US as Lopez is Puerto Rican American and Puerto Rico, of course, has a predominantly African diasporic population as a result of the trade of African slaves in the Caribbean and the Americas. Julio and Miles, like the mainstream media, understand Lopez as Latina and not Black – though of course many African Caribbeans are both Black and Latino/a.

16 Such racist sexualized mythology about Black female bodies in nineteenth-century European "anthropology," which sought to prove racial superiority through phenotype, is documented in prose and photography in Willis and Williams (2002), *The Black Female Body*.

17 See Carpio (2008) for an extended argument on the use of humor in African American literature, stand-up comedy, and visual art as a resistance to the legacy of slavery. Beyond merely flipping pain into humor, Carpio argues that invoking racist stereotypes only to turn them on their head can be a form of resistance to those very stereotypes.

18 This is an important point as the study of the dozens and ritual insult has been dominated by analysis of male Black exchanges (often analyzed by male researchers) until recently (Morgan, 2002; Smitherman, 2006).

19 *I'ma*, an AAL feature for first person future action, represents a complicated morphological transformation from the DAE "I'm going to."

20 I avoid unquoted uses of the word itself in my own writing to respect those who may find such uses offensive.

21 Smitherman (1977) calls the African American practice of reversing and repurposing meanings *semantic inversion*.

22 Smitherman (2006) lists eight meanings of "nigga" depending on speaker and context, from positive, to neutral, to negative, with the derogatory being "nigger" with the "r" realized.

23 Such *marking* through White phonology is explored over a century of Black comedy in Rickford and Rickford (2000).

24 Again see Carpio (2008), who forwards this argument through deft analysis of Black humor over the centuries.

25 Although I remain focused on the N-words here, it is worth noting that Juan's statement, "Yo legs is hella ashy" represents AAL phonology ("yo" for "your" – called r-vocalization), generalized verb agreement with "is" for "are", and the lexical item "ashy."

26 Jacobs (1999), Kennedy (2002), and Smitherman (1977) are examples of scholarship on the N-words.

27 Alim (2006) and Spears (1998) give brief mention of the N-words being used across ethnicity, though this is not the focus of either work and neither work includes multiple examples or youth understandings of this use.

28 See Zhou (2001) for a discussion of African American population trends in the urban United States.

29 This is an internalized shame about AAL that continues to haunt many in the African American community (Baugh, 1999; Rickford and Rickford, 2000).

30 See Rickford, Sweetland, and Rickford (2004) for a topic-coded bibliography of AAL and other Englishes in education. See Godley *et al.* (2006) for an excellent article reviewing research-based pedagogical applications of AAL. The research of Arnetha Ball (1995, 1999) investigates the ways AAL grammar, lexicon, and rhetorical structures carry into the writing of AAL-speaking students. See Alim (2004) for research showing the development of research and writing skills using the AAL of students as a foundation and Lee (1995) for an example of pedagogical and curricular approaches to using AAL as a resource for literary analysis.

INTERLUDE: ON ORAL LANGUAGE USE, RESEARCH, AND TEACHING IN MULTIETHNIC SCHOOLS

1 For examples of this growing scholarship at the edge of sociolinguistics, linguistic anthropology, and education see Guerra (2004), who describes such plurality as *nomadic consciousness* allowing social actors to navigate disparate cultural domains. Also see Carter's (2005) work with Latino/a and Black youth. Though not focused on language, Carter calls for fostering *multicultural navigators* who can move fluidly across lines of difference. In Alim's (2004) research on AAL use among youth he labels the abilities of AAL speakers to shift English varieties, *linguistic flexibility.*

2 I use these three theorists because the many following decades of thinking about teaching and curriculum in general, and critical, social justice learning in particular, are in large part a working out of this thinking.

3 This process of coming to themes is the first major stage in Freire's (1970) pedagogy called *thematic investigations.*

5   "YOU REP WHAT YOU'RE FROM": TEXTING IDENTITIES IN MULTIETHNIC YOUTH SPACE

1 See Bakhtin (1981) and Vygotsky (1978) for theoretical discussions of the social life of language.

2 These multimodal forms of writing are challenging the primacy of dominant print literacy, though they are in no way new. Anzaldúa (1987) and Baca (2008) have shown such writing at the heart of Mesoamerican written communication systems that were systematically destroyed by conquistadors in favor of alphabetized print dominance.

3 "Little City Killing Zone" had been a local "street" name for South Vista for over a decade, referring to the high numbers of homicides each year.

4 It is worthy of note that Ela's backpack explicitly indexed gender. Other forms of text, like the flowed texts of rap, were mainly male spaces in my observations. While I will show young men indexing gender in flowed texts, it would be a mistake to assume young women, like Ela, didn't also find public ways to make gender claims through text.

5 R-vocalization (in Ela's text, *for→fo*) represents an "r" sound vocalized into a vowel sound following a vowel. See Green (2002) for a full account of r-vocalization.

6 As Baugh and Smitherman (2007) have noted, the counter spellings of AAL and Hip Hop culture are often conscious acts of linguistic identity.

7 In Kirkland's (2009) work on tattoos among Black men he discusses such inked literacy, body politics, and their potential for humanized literacy learning.

8 I build here on Hymes' (1972) notion of *speech acts* and Heath's (1983) complementary notion of *literacy events* as what speakers and writers and their audiences are trying to achieve through particular uses of language within the community norms of those uses of language.

9 The title of this section is a text message I received from Rochelle in July of 2007. It includes AAL phonology in consonant cluster reduction ("was" for "what's) and consonant replacements ("dis" for "this" and "doin" for "doing").

10 These text messaging, social networking, and email exchanges have continued with many of the youth three years after the study.

11 I, too, participated in resistant spellings and AAL grammar, phonology, and lexicon in my texting. Although this participation was authentic and was part of my text messaging and emailing outside the research, I did not introduce features I had not already seen in particular youths' texts.

12 I use italics throughout text examples in this chapter to highlight features of AAL and other language varieties, youth and Hip Hop lexicon, eye dialect, and ethnic or local urban affiliations. I preserve all youth spelling, capitalization, and punctuation.

13 See Smitherman (2006) for a relatively current AAL lexicon including "Yo" and "Boy."

14 This is a common consonant replacement of AAL and other non-dominant Englishes, noted as ð→d.

15 This is noted in linguistics as the consonant replacement ŋ→n. Features common to AAL and other Englishes were marked as AAL at South Vista.

16 It is important to note that my numerous email and text message exchanges with Carla and Gloria contained few features of AAL, though they did participate in resistant orthography and hyper-efficiency. This follows my previous

discussions of the lack of Spanish use by African American and Pacific Islander young women and the relative lack of AAL use by Latinas as related to the lack of speakers of these languages in their close social networks.

17 I realize some may read such a reference as stereotypical, as replacing one struggling Black mother with another, though I did not experience the comparison that way. Rather, my thoughts of Mama and my thoughts of Rochelle's mother centered on the role of Black women and Black mothers as holding culture and family together despite the best efforts of dominant society to tear them apart.

18 This is a feature AAL shares with non-dominant varieties of southern White speech, though it was marked as AAL in South Vista (Rickford and Rickford, 2000).

19 This is noted as the consonant replacement $\theta \rightarrow$ t.

20 The technology of cell phones, including cell phone keyboards used to text message, has changed significantly since 2007. Current programs for spell checking as well as full keyboards will undoubtedly influence the types of vernacular language youth employ in texting, making representations of the vernacular that do remain all the more resistant and conscious.

21 According to Chang's (2005) thorough history, the roots of Hip Hop music and rapping began in Jamaica (itself deeply influenced by both African and African American musical traditions), though the craft and culture grew up in mixed Caribbean and African American communities NYC.

22 Again, *Hyphy* was a local metro area dance, rap style, and counter-cultural movement.

23 I attempt to preserve the rhyme and rhythm of Larul's raps, though due to changes in names some are lost.

24 Such toasting, a narrative form centered on stories boasting of amazing talents and feats, is recognized as a seminal feature of the African American storytelling and lyrical tradition (Green, 2002; Rickford and Rickford, 2000).

25 The fact that this is at once a flowed and delivered text points to the interrelationship of various sorts of identity texts in the youth space of South Vista.

26 See Chapter 4 for a complete discussion of the semantics and pragmatics of the N-words at South Vista.

27 A significant amount of rap, most of it not commercially successful and not played on the radio, does not participate in these themes of female subjection and material success as the primary form of success. In fact, much of this "underground" Hip Hop actively resists such themes. Youth-authored flows like Larul's "New Root" show this other, prevalent genre of rap lyrics that

does not often achieve the commercial success, or media coverage, of violent and misogynistic rap. See Alim (2006), Alim, Ibrahim, and Pennycook (2009), Chang (2005), and Smitherman (2006) for discussions and examples of crucially conscious Hip Hop and the tensions between various Hip Hop cultures.

28 Again, see Smitherman (2006) for a critical discussion of the cultural semantics of "bitch" and "ho" as importantly dependent on user and cultural context.

29 As Bakhtin (1981) illuminated more than eighty years ago, the distinction between form and content is false, as each informs the other in the dialogic construction of meaning. I separate them here for purposes of analysis.

30 For theoretical discussions from new literacies perspectives challenging the separation and superiority of orality over literacy, see de Certeau (1984), Street (1984), Collins & Blot (2003), and Paris and Kirkland (2011).

31 See Dyson (2005) and Fisher (2005) for a discussion of the ways spoken word and other youth forms blur the oral/written dichotomy and offer possibilities for literacy learning and research.

32 The burgeoning research on Hip Hop pedagogy in the United States includes Alim (2004, 2006), Alim and Baugh (2007), Hill (2009), Kirkland (2008), Mahiri (2001), Morell (2003), Morell and Duncan-Andrade (2002), and Smitherman (2006).

33 See Alim, Ibrahim, and Pennycook (2009) for essays on Hip Hop in global perspective.

34 Delpit (1995) uses the term *culture of power* to describe the explicit and implicit codes of language use and other cultural behaviors students need to access power in schools and society. She argues that students of color are not often given explicit instruction on the differences between what languages and behaviors are accepted and privileged in their home and community and those accepted and privileged in schools and dominant society.

35 Also see Kirkland (2008) for a discussion of the third space concept in English pedagogy.

36 This sort of dialogic teaching, learning, and production echoes Freire's (1970) notions of pedagogy and Anzaldúa's (1987) visions of linguistic and cultural hybridity.

37 See Lunsford (2007) for an essay arguing that the changing rhetorics and structures of writing with the advent of digital literacies require new approaches to conceptualizing and teaching writing.

38 See Ball (1995, 1999) for discourse analysis of the connections between oral and written communication for African American AAL-speaking students.

39 Again, Rickford, Sweetland, and Rickford (2004) provide an excellent bibliography of research on AAL and other Englishes in education, and Godley *et al.* (2006) review pedagogical applications for contrasting AAL and DAE in the classroom.

40 This sort of problem posing using the experiences and practices of students as resources for learning is at the heart of progressive (Dewey, 1938) and critical theory (Freire, 1970).

6   MAKING SCHOOL *GO*: RE-VISIONING SCHOOL
     FOR PLURALISM

1 Many of these critiques have come from advocates of critical multicultural education (see Banks, 1993; Sleeter, 1996). Others have come more broadly from critical theorists of education (notably, Giroux, 1988). This critique has also been leveled by critical race theorists of education (see the work of Ladson-Billings, 1995, 2006). A massive body of scholarship also shows this mainstreaming or transitioning goal of schooling in language and literacy education (see Heath, 1983; Romaine, 1995; Smitherman, 1977; Valdés, 1996, among many others).

2 See Heath (1992) for a thorough discussion of the political rhetoric and policy around linguistic pluralism during the founding and early years of the United States.

3 Dewey (1938), Freire (1970), Vygotsky (1978) and many others afterward begin from this basic position. Sociocultural learning theory (Cole, 1996; Rogoff, 2003; Wenger, 1999) and New Literacy theory (Street, 1984; Collins and Blot, 2003) also take up this basic position.

4 See Banks (1993), Sleeter (1996), and Ladson-Billings (1995) as examples.

5 See Cochran-Smith (1995) and Paris and Ball (2009) for discussions of the role of teacher inquiry in teacher training for multiethnic contexts.

6 See Chapter 4 for a discussion envisioning such curriculum development at South Vista High.

APPENDIX: NOTES ON METHODOLOGY IN CULTURAL
STUDIES OF LANGUAGE ACROSS DIFFERENCE

1 See Fairclough (2001a, 2001b) for thinking on CDA as a theoretical and methodological approach to studying oral and written language.

2 This tradition stretches back into the 1960s when sociolinguistics as a recognized field in the US emerged in large part from the work of William Labov (1972). Labov and his collaborators sought to prove the systematicity of AAL syntax, morphology, and grammar by showing that AAL features varied systematically by, among other things, social categories of speaker and interlocutor.

3 See Baugh and Smitherman (2007) and Alim (2006) for more on such conscious resistant spelling in AAL and Hip Hop writing.

4 Models of contemporary approaches to the study of language choice and code-switching in multilingual contexts again include Myers-Scotton and Bolonyai (2001) from their work in multilingual Kenya, and Wei, Milroy, and Ching (2000) in bilingual Chinese communities in Britain.

5 My most powerful influences in ethnography and qualitative methodology are Geertz (1973), Peshkin (1993), and Pope (2001).

6 Most notable among the methodologists I lean on to engage in linguistic anthropological orientations to language in social and cultural life are Hymes (1972), Zentella (1997) and Goodwin (2002).

7 The sociolinguistic interview was in large part developed by Labov (1984). This basic methodology has been pushed in the research literature to foreground the fact that the linguistic repertoire and other social categories (e.g., race, gender) of the interviewer have a major effect on the representativeness of language samples. So, for instance, my Black biracial status and relative comfort with AAL and participation in Black culture were positives in this regard, while my participation in DAE, my age, and my biracial status were relative negatives. See Alim (2004) and Rickford and McNair-Knox (1994) for research on interviewer effect in the quantitative variationist sociolinguistic study of AAL features.

8 Briggs (1986) long ago described the need for ethnographic and social language interviews to be based in the cultural and linguistic context of the participants, even linking cultural activities to the elicitation of valid responses.

9 In both the interview data as well as other forms of data I gathered at South Vista, my own comfort and training in AAL made my linguistic focus on AAL more intense than my linguistic focus on other languages in the study as a whole. My limited proficiency in Spanish and lack of ability in Samoan, and Hindi, of course, limited the sorts of data gathering and analysis I could engage in with those languages. I was unwilling, however, to ignore the important role of Spanish and Pacific Islander languages and believe my findings about all the languages spoken by the youth of South Vista are valuable contributions to the severely underdeveloped US research literature on language across difference in changing multiethnic and multilingual schools.

10 See Emerson, Fretz, and Shaw (1995) for a thorough treatment of techniques and rationales for fieldnotes in studies of culture. The recording of linguistic content in fieldnotes has received far less attention in the methodology literature, and I hope my methodology can offer some example in this regard.

11 One caution to engaging in transdisciplinary methodologies is the possibility that researchers borrow from methods they know little about – in terms of the intellectual history or the day-to-day techniques of collection and analysis. I have been fortunate to have sustained training in each of the social language, educational, and cultural fields I draw on in my work.

References

Alim, H. S. (2004). *You know my steez: An ethnographic and sociolinguistic study of a black American speech community*. Durham, NC: Duke University Press.

Alim, H. S. (2006). *Roc the mic right: The language of hip hop culture*. New York: Routledge.

Alim, H. S., and Baugh, J. (eds.) (2007). *Talkin Black talk: Language, education, and social change*. New York: Teachers College Press.

Alim, H. S., Ibrahim, A., and Pennycook, A. (eds.) (2009). *Global linguistic flows: Hip hop cultures, youth identities, and the politics of language*. London: Routledge.

Anzaldúa, G. (1987, 1999). *Borderlands/La frontera: The new mestiza*. San Francisco: Aunt Lute Books.

Baca, D. (2008). *Mestiz@ scripts, digital migrations and the territories of writing*. Hampshire, England: Palgrave Macmillan.

Bakhtin, M. M. (1981). Discourse in the novel. In M. Holquist (ed.), *The dialogic imagination: Four essays* (pp. 257–422). Austin, TX: University of Texas Press.

Ball, A. (1995). Text design patterns in the writing of urban African American students: Teaching to the cultural strengths of students in multicultural settings. *Urban Education* **30**(3), 253–89.

Ball, A. (1999). Evaluating the writing of culturally and linguistically diverse students: The case of the African American vernacular English speaker. In C. Cooper and L. Odell (eds.), *Evaluating writing* (pp. 225–48). Urbana, IL: National Council of Teachers of English.

Ball, A. (ed.) (2006). *With more deliberate speed: Achieving equity and excellence in education – realizing the full potential of Brown V. Board of Education*. National Society for the Study of Education. Malden, MA: Blackwell.

Banks, J. (1993). The canon debate, knowledge construction, and multicultural education. *Educational Researcher* **22**(5), 4–14.

Baugh, J. (1983). *Black street speech*. Austin, TX: University of Texas Press.

Baugh, J. (1999). *Out of the mouths of slaves: African American Language and educational malpractice*. Austin, TX: University of Texas Press.

Baugh, J., and Smitherman, G. (2007). Linguistic emancipation in global perspective. In Alim and Baugh (eds.), pp. 115–32.

Bhahba, H. K. (1994). *The location of culture*. London: Routledge.

Bonner, D. M. (2004). Garifuna children's language shame: Ethnic stereotypes, national affiliation, and transnational immigration as factors in language choice in Southern Belize. *Language in Society* **30**(1), 81–96.

Briggs, C. H. (1986). *Learning how to ask: A sociolinguistic appraisal of the role of the interview in social science research*. New York: Cambridge University Press.

Bucholtz, M., and Hall, K. (2004). Language and identity. In A. Duranti (ed.), *A Companion to Linguistic Anthropology* (pp. 369–94). Malden, MA: Blackwell.

Burke, K. (1969). *A rhetoric of motives*. Berkeley, CA: University of California Press.

Carpio, G. (2008). *Laughing fit to kill: Black humor in the fictions of slavery*. New York: Oxford University Press.

Carter, P. (2005). *Keepin it real: School success beyond black and white*. New York: Oxford University Press.

Chang, J. (2005). *Can't stop, won't stop: The history of the hip hop generation*. New York: Picador.

Charmaz, K. (2005). Grounded theory in the 21st century. In N. K. Denzin and Y. S. Lincoln (eds.), *The Sage handbook of qualitative research* (pp. 507–35). Thousand Oaks, CA: Sage Publications.

Cintron, R. (1997). *Angel's town: Chero ways, gang life, and the rhetorics of the everyday*. Boston, MA: Beacon.

Cisneros, S. (1989). *The house on Mango Street*. New York: Vintage Books.

Cochran-Smith, M. (1995). Color blindness and basket making are not the answers: Confronting dilemmas of race, culture and language diversity in teacher education. *American Educational Research Journal* **32**(3), 493–522.

Cole, M. (1996). *Cultural psychology: A once and future discipline*. Harvard University Press.

Collins, J., and Blot, R. (2003). *Literacy and literacies: Texts, power, and identity*. Cambridge University Press.

Collins, P. H. (2004). *Black sexual politics: African Americans, gender, and the new racism*. New York: Routledge.

Crystal, D. (2000). *Language death*. Cambridge University Press.

de Certeau, M. (1984). *The practice of everyday life*. Berkeley, CA: University of California Press.

Delpit, L. (1995). The silenced dialogue. In *Other people's children: Cultural conflict in the classroom* (pp. 21–47). New York: New Press.

Dewey, J. (1938). *Experience and education.* New York: Touchstone.

Dubois, W. E. B. (1903, 1965). *The souls of black folk.* New York: Avon Books.

Dyson, A. H. (2005). Crafting "the humble prose of living": Rethinking oral/written relations in the echoes of spoken word. *English Education* 37(2), 149–64.

Eckert, P. (1989). The whole woman: sex and gender differences in variation. *Language Variation and Change* 1, 245–67.

Eisenhart, M., and Howe, K. (1992). Validity in educational research. In M. D. LeCompte, W. Millroy, and J. Preissle (eds.), *Handbook of qualitative research in education* (pp. 643–80). San Diego: Academic Press.

Emerson, R., Fretz, R., and Shaw, L. (1995). *Writing ethnographic fieldnotes.* University of Chicago Press.

Fairclough, N. (2001a). *Language and power.* Essex: Pearson Education Limited.

Fairclough, N. (2001b). Critical discourse analysis as a method in social scientific research. In R. Wodak and M. Meyer (eds.), *Methods of Critical Discourse Analysis* (pp. 121–38). London: Sage Publications.

Fisher, M. (2005). From the coffee house to the school house: The promise of spoken work poetry in school contexts. *English Education* 37(2), 115–31.

Fishman, J. A. (1965). Who speaks what language to whom and when? *La Linguistique* 2, 67–88.

Fishman, J. A. (1991). *Reversing language shift.* Clevedon, UK: Multilingual Matters.

Fought, C. (2006). *Language and ethnicity.* Cambridge University Press.

Freire, P. (1970). *Pedagogy of the oppressed.* New York: Continuum.

Gal, S. (1991). Between speech and silence: Problematics of research on language and gender. In M. DiLeonardo (ed.), *Gender at the crossroads of knowledge: Feminist anthropology in the postmodern era* (pp. 175–203). Berkeley, CA: University of California Press.

Game, T. (2005). How we do. On *The Documentary* [CD]. Los Angeles: G Unit Records.

Garcia, E. (1993). Language, culture, and education. *Review of Research in Education* 19, 51–98.

Gee, J. (1999). What is literacy? In C. Mitchell and K. Weiler (eds.), *Reviewing literacy: Culture and the discourse of the other* (pp. 3–11). Westport, CT: Bergin and Garvin.

Gee, J. (2001). Identity as an analytic lens for research in education. In W. Secada (ed.), *Review of Research in Education,* 25 (pp. 99–125). Washington, DC: American Educational Research Association.

Geertz, C. (1973). *The interpretation of cultures*. New York: Basic Books.

Gifford, B., and Valdés, G. (2006). The linguistic isolation of Hispanic students in California's public schools. In Ball (ed.), pp. 125–54.

Giroux, H. (1988). *Teachers as intellectuals: Toward a critical pedagogy of learning*. Westport, CT: Bergin and Garvey.

Godley, A., Sweetland, J., Wheeler, R., Minnici, A., and Carpenter, B. (2006). Preparing teachers for dialectally diverse classrooms. *Educational Researcher* 35(8), 30–38.

Goodwin, M. (1980). He-said-she-said: Formal cultural procedures for the construction of a gossip dispute activity. *American Ethnologist* 7, 674–95.

Goodwin, M. (1990). *He-said-she-said: Talk as social organization among black children*. Bloomington, IN: Indiana University Press.

Goodwin, M. (2002). Exclusion in girls' play groups: Ethnographic analysis of language practices on the playground. *Human Development* 45, 392–415.

Green, L. (2002). *African American English: A linguistic introduction*. Cambridge University Press.

Guba, E., and Lincoln, Y. (2005). Paradigmatic controversies, contradictions, and emerging confluences. In N. K. Denzin and Y. S. Lincoln (eds.), *The Sage handbook of qualitative research* (pp. 191–215). Thousand Oaks, CA: Sage Publications.

Guerra, J. (1998). *Close to home: Oral and literate practices in a transnational Mexicano community*. New York: Teachers College Press.

Guerra, J. (2004). Putting literacy in its place: Nomadic consciousness and the practice of transcultural repositioning. In C. Gutiérrez-Jones (ed.), *Rebellious reading: The dynamics of Chicana/o cultural literacy* (pp. 96–123). Santa Barbara, CA: University of California at Santa Barbara Press.

Gutiérrez, K. (2008). Developing a sociocritical literacy in the third space. *Reading Research Quarterly* 43(2), 148–64.

Gutiérrez, K., and Rogoff, B. (2003). Cultural ways of learning. *Educational Researcher* 35(5), 19–25.

Gutiérrez, K., Baquedano-Lopez, P., Alvarez, H., and Chiu, M. (1999). Building a culture of collaboration through hybrid language practices. *Theory Into Practice* 38, 87–93.

Hall, S. (1988). New ethnicities. In A. Rattansi and J. Donald (eds.), *"Race," Culture, and Difference* (pp. 252–59). London: Sage/The Open University.

Hall, S., Hubert, D., and Thompson, K. (eds.) (1996). *Modernity: An introduction to modern societies*. London: Blackwell.

Hansberry, L. (1959, 2002). *A raisin in the sun*. New York: Random House.

Harris, R. (2006). *New ethnicities and language use*. New York: Palgrave Macmillan.

Heath, S. B. (1983). *Ways with words*. New York: Cambridge University Press.

Heath, S. B. (1992). Why no official tongue? In J. Crawford (ed.), *A source book on the official English controversy* (pp. 20–32). University of Chicago Press.

Hill, J. (2001). Language, race and white public space. In A. Duranti (ed.), *Linguistic anthropology: A reader* (pp. 450–64). Oxford, UK: Blackwell.

Hill, M. L. (2009). *Beats, rhymes and classroom life: Hip-hop pedagogy and the politics of identity*. New York: Teachers College Press.

Howe, K. R. (2009). Epistemology, methodology, and education sciences: Positivist dogmas, rhetoric, and the education science question. *Educational Researcher* **38**(6), 428–40.

Hymes, D. (1972). Models of the interaction of language and social life. In J. Gumperz and D. Hymes (eds.), *Directions in sociolinguistics: The ethnography of communication* (pp. 35–71). New York, NY: Holt, Rinehart and Winston.

Irizarry, J. (2011) *The Latinization of US schools: Successful teaching and learning in shifting cultural contexts*. Boulder, CO: Paradigm.

Jacobs, B. (1999). *Race manners*. New York: Arcade Publishing.

Jordan, J. (1985). Nobody mean more to me than you, and the future life of Willie Jordan. In *On call: political essays* (pp. 157–72). Boston, MA: South End.

Jørgensen, J. N. (2008). Polylingual languaging around and among children and adolescents. *International Journal of Multilingualism* **5**(3), 161–76.

Kennedy, R. (2002). *Nigger: The strange career of a troublesome word*. New York: Pantheon Books.

Kirkland, D. (2008). The rose that grew from concrete: Postmodern blackness and new English education. *English Journal* **97**(5), 69–75.

Kirkland, D. (2009). The skin we ink: Tattoos, literacy, and a new English education. *English Education* **41**(4), 375–95.

Klein, H. (2004). *A population history of the United States*. Cambridge University Press.

Kozol, J. (2005) Still separate, still unequal: America's educational apartheid. *Harpers Magazine*, **311**(1864), September 1.

Labov, W. (1972). *Language in the inner city*. Philadelphia, PA: University of Pennsylvania Press.

Labov, W. (1984). Field methods of the project on linguistic change and variation. In J. Baugh and J. Sherzer (eds.), *Language in use: Readings in sociolinguistics*. Englewood Cliffs, NJ: Prentice Hall.

Ladson-Billings, G. (1995). Toward a theory of culturally relevant pedagogy. *American Educational Research Journal* **32**(3), 465–91.

Ladson-Billings, G. (2006). The meaning of Brown ... for now. In Ball (ed.), pp. 298–313.

Landry, D., and MacLean, G. (1996). *The Spivak reader.* New York: Routledge.

Lee, C. D. (1995). A culturally based cognitive apprenticeship: Teaching African American high school students skills in literary interpretation. *Reading Research Quarterly* **30**(4), 608–30.

Lee, S. (2002). Learning "America": Hmong American high school students. *Education and Urban Society* **34**(2), 233–46.

Le Page, R. B., and Tabouret-Keller, A. (1985). *Acts of identity.* Cambridge University Press.

Lippi-Green, R. (1997). *English with an accent: Language, ideology, and discrimination in the United States.* New York: Routledge.

Lunsford, A. (2004). Towards a Mestiza rhetoric: Gloria Anzaldúa on composition and postcoloniality. In A. Lunsford and L. Ouzgame (eds.), *Crossing borderlands: composition and postcolonial studies* (pp. 33–66). University of Pittsburg Press.

Lunsford, A. (2007). *Writing matters: Rhetoric in public and private lives.* Athens: University of Georgia Press.

Mahiri, J. (2001). Pop culture pedagogy and the end(s) of school. *Journal of Adolescent and Adult Literacy* **44**(4), 382–85.

Massey, D. (2001). Residential segregation and neighborhood conditions in US metropolitan areas. In Smelser, Wilson, and Mitchell (eds.), pp. 391–434.

Moje, E. B., Ciechanowski, K. M., Kramer, K., Ellis, L., Carrillo, R., and Collazo, T. (2004). Working toward third space in content area literacy: An examination of everyday funds of knowledge and discourse. *Reading Research Quarterly* **39**(1), 38–70.

Moll, L. (1992). Literacy research in community and classrooms: A sociocultural approach. In R. Beach, J. L. Green, M. L. Kamil, and T. Shanahan (eds.), *Multidisciplinary perspectives in literacy research* (pp. 211–44). Urbana, IL : National Conference on Research in English and National Council of Teachers of English.

Moll, L., and Gonzalez, N. (1994). Lessons from research with language minority children. *Journal of Reading Behavior* **26**(4), 23–41.

Morgan, M. (2002). *Language, discourse and power in African American culture.* Cambridge University Press.

Morrell, E. (2003). Toward a critical pedagogy of popular culture: Literacy development among urban youth. *Journal of Adolescent and Adult Literacy* **46**(1), 72–77.

Morrell, E. (2004). *Becoming critical researchers: Literacy and empowerment for urban youth*. New York: Peter Lang.

Morrell, E., and Duncan-Andrade, J. (2002). Promoting academic literacy with urban youth through engaging in hip-hop culture. *English Journal* **91**(6), 88–92.

Myers-Scotton, C., and Bolonyai, A. (2001). Calculating speakers: Codeswitchers in a rational choice model. *Language in Society* **30**(1), 1–28.

Olsen, L. (1997). Made in America: Immigrant students in our public schools. New York: The New Press.

Paris, D., and Ball, A. (2009). Teacher knowledge in culturally and linguistically complex classrooms: Lessons from the golden age and beyond. In L. M. Morrow, R. Rueda, and D. Lapp (eds.), *Handbook of research on literacy instruction: Issues of diversity, policy, and equity* (pp. 379–95). New York: Guilford Publications.

Paris, D., and Kirkland, D. E. (2011). "The consciousness of the verbal artist": Understanding vernacular literacies in digital and embodied spaces. In V. Kinloch (ed.), *Urban literacies: Critical perspectives on language, learning, and community* (pp. 177–94). New York: Teachers College Press.

Peshkin, A. (1993). The goodness of qualitative research. *Educational Researcher*, **22**(2), 23–29.

Pope, D. (2001). *Doing school: How we are creating a generation of stressed out, materialistic, and miseducated students*. New Haven, CT: Yale University Press.

Pratt, M. L. (1987). Linguistic utopias. In N. Fabb, D. Attridge, A. Durant, and C. MacCabe (eds.), *The linguistics of writing: Arguments between language and literature* (pp. 48–56). Manchester University Press.

Pratt, M. L. (1991). Arts of the contact zone. *Profession* **91**, 33–40.

Rampton, B. (1995). *Crossing: Language and ethnicity among adolescents*. New York: Longman.

Rampton, B. (1998). Language crossing and the redefinition of reality. In P. Auer (ed.), *Code switching in conversation: Language, interaction and identity* (pp. 290–317). London: Routledge.

Rampton, B. (2006). *Language in late modernity: Interaction in an urban school*. Cambridge University Press.

Rickford, J., and McNair-Knox, F. (1994). Addressee- and topic-influenced style shift: A quantitative sociolinguistic study. In D. Biber and E. Finegan (eds.), *Sociolinguistic perspectives on register* (pp. 235–75). New York: Oxford University Press.

Rickford, J., and Rickford, R. (2000). *Spoken soul: The story of black English*. New York: John Wiley and Sons.

Rickford, J., Sweetland, J., and Rickford, A. (2004). African American English and other vernaculars in education: A topic-coded bibliography. *Journal of English Linguistics* **32**(3), 230–320.

Rogoff, B. (2003). *The cultural nature of human development.* New York: Oxford University Press.

Romaine, S. (1995). Bilingualism and education. In *Bilingualism* (pp. 241–87). Malden, MA: Blackwell.

Rose, M. (1989). *Lives on the boundary.* New York: Penguin Books.

Sinclair, U. (1906, 1985). *The jungle.* New York: Penguin Books.

Sleeter, C. (1996). *Multicultural education as social activism.* New York: State University of New York Press.

Smelser, N., Wilson, J., and Mitchell, F. (eds.) (2001). *American becoming: Racial trends and their consequences.* Washington, DC: National Academies Press.

Smitherman, G. (1977). *Talkin and testifyin.* Detroit, IL: Wayne State University Press.

Smitherman, G. (2006). *Word from the mother: Language and African Americans.* New York: Routledge.

Spears, A. (1998). African-American language use: Ideology and so-called obscenity. In S. Mufwene, J. Rickford, G. Bailey, and J. Baugh (eds.) *African American English: Structure, History, Use* (pp. 226–50). New York: Routledge.

Spivak, G. (1989). *A critique of postcolonial reason: Toward a history of the vanishing present.* Cambridge: Harvard University Press.

Street, B. (1984). *Literacy in theory and practice.* New York: Cambridge University Press.

Stritikus, T., and Nguyen, D. (2007). Strategic transformation: Cultural and gender identity negotiation in first generation Vietnamese youth. *American Educational Research Journal* **44** (4), 853–96.

Tyler, R. (1949). *The basic principles of curriculum and instruction.* The University of Chicago Press.

Valdés, G. (1996). *Con respeto: Bridging the distances between culturally diverse families and schools.* New York: Teachers College Press.

Valdés, G., and Figueroa, R. A. (1994). The measurement of bilingualism. In *Bilingualism and Testing: A Special Case of Bias* (pp. 29–67). Norwood, NJ: Ablex.

Vygotsky, L. S. (1978). *Mind in society.* Cambridge, MA: Harvard University Press.

Wei, L., Milroy, M., and Ching, P. S. (2001). A two-step sociolinguistic analysis of code-switching and language choice: The example of a bilingual

Chinese community in Britain. In L. Wei (ed.), *The bilingualism reader.* New York: Routledge.

Wenger, E. (1999). *Communities of practice: learning, meaning, and identity.* New York: Cambridge University Press.

Willis, D., and Williams, C. (2002). *The black female body: A photographic history.* Philadelphia, PA: Temple University Press.

Wilson, A. (2000). Aunt Ester's children: A century onstage. *The New York Times,* April 23.

Zentella, A. C. (1997). *Growing up bilingual.* Oxford, UK: Blackwell.

Zhou, M. (2001). Contemporary immigration and the dynamics of race and ethnicity. In Smelser, Wilson, and Mitchell (eds.), pp. 200–42.

Index